MW00614486

HOW TO LEARN
A FOREIGN LANGUAGE

by
Paul Pimsleur, Ph.D.

PIMSLEUR LANGUAGE PROGRAMS
New York   London   Toronto   Sydney   New Delhi

PIMSLEUR

Pimsleur Language Programs
Simon & Schuster Audio
30 Monument Square
Concord, MA 01742

Pimsleur Language Programs
Simon & Schuster Audio
1230 Avenue of the Americas
New York, NY 10020

First Hardcover Edition & E-book Edition Copyright © 2013
Cengage Learning

All rights reserved,
including the right to reproduce
this book or portions thereof
in any form whatsoever.

Pimsleur® is an imprint of Simon & Schuster Audio,
a division of Simon & Schuster, Inc. All rights reserved.
PIMSLEUR® is a registered trademark of Beverly Pimsleur,
used by Simon & Schuster under exclusive license.

First Edition Copyright © 1980 Heinle & Heinle Publishers, Inc.

Manufactured in the United States of America.

Library of Congress Cataloging-in-Publication data is available.

ISBN 978-1-4423-6902-3 (hardcover)
ISBN 978-1-4423-6903-0 (ebook)

For Jean

Table of Contents

Foreword

For me, this is the perfect book on learning a new language.

It is all the things most language learning tools are not. It's direct, full of useful pearls of wisdom that are easily incorporated into one's day-to-day study of a new language. It's clear and well written, and nowhere does "academic-speak" sneak into the text.

Paul Pimsleur's theories, as expressed in *How to Learn a Foreign Language,* are deceptively simple. In his own teaching, Dr. Pimsleur saw students repeatedly failing and being turned off of what to him was the most exciting challenge in the world: learning a new language.

This book speaks equally to the different kinds of would-be language learners—from those who thought themselves scarred for life by high school Spanish hell to the more confident learners who want to approach the full range of different languages. You'll be surprised at the Foreign Service Institute's (FSI's) grouping of "easy" to "hard" languages: what language ranks where isn't entirely obvious.

Paul Pimsleur was very direct in his advice on what to look for in a teacher: when the classroom experience is not going to help you learn and when it is, when you're within your rights to object to your time being wasted by methods that aren't going to teach you anything.

A lot of what I've come to know as the Pimsleur Method is developed from the ground up in this book.

As Pimsleur walks you step-by-step through his straightforward advice on how to learn a language, so he sets out the principles of the Pimsleur Method, answering many of the questions I've had about the reasoning behind the program. By the end of this short book, you've gotten the benefit of his years of experience and the results of his research that led to defining the behaviors proven to result in your learning a new language more easily.

I'm also lucky to be in frequent contact with Dr. Pimsleur's wife, Beverly, and his daughter, Julia, both of whom cheer us on in spreading the word about Pimsleur. As importantly, they each keep Paul Pimsleur from becoming a lifeless statue, constantly providing insights and anecdotes about Pimsleur that enable us to think of him as present in our daily business.

It has been some thirty-seven years since Paul Pimsleur died of a heart attack while he was teaching at the Sorbonne in Paris. His wife, Beverly Pimsleur, brought the manuscript of this book to Charles Heinle, the original publisher, and he published it in 1980. It was Charles's wife, Beverly Heinle, Pimsleur Language Programs editor-in-chief, who suggested we republish it as part of our fiftieth anniversary celebration in 2013.

The statistics and other reference materials are more than thirty years old, but they remain directionally correct—the underlying point would be the same if they were all translated to 2013 values.

I only wish this edition could reflect what Dr. Pimsleur would have done with all of the new technology that has emerged in the ensuing thirty years. He was always in the forefront: in the 1960s he was responsible for developing the first computerized language laboratory at Ohio State University, where he set up a venture with Ohio Bell Telephone Company that enabled students to learn at their own pace, dialing in directly to hear preprogrammed tapes. I can't help but think he'd admire the revolutionary Course Manager App we've developed.

To celebrate the fiftieth anniversary of the Pimsleur programs, we are republishing Paul Pimsleur's original *How to Learn a Foreign Language*. It is astonishing how it has stood the test of time.

The mechanical delivery systems have changed: for cassettes, records, and tape recorders, you can now read in CDs and downloads. The political alignments in Appendix 1, "Languages of the World," have changed, but the languages remain. The number of speakers listed in Table 2, "The Twelve Most Widely Spoken Languages," has increased, and the ranking order of the languages fluctuates, but they are still the most widely spoken.

And all the rest holds true: Paul's wisdom is as valuable today as it was when it was originally published.

Robert Paris Riger

Paul Pimsleur's Life and Career

Paul Pimsleur (October 17, 1927–June 22, 1976) was a scholar in the field of applied linguistics. He developed the Pimsleur language learning system, which, along with his many publications, had a significant effect on theories of language learning and teaching.

Paul Pimsleur was born in New York City and grew up in the Bronx. His father, Solomon Pimsleur, was from France and a composer of music; his American-born mother was a librarian at Columbia University.

Dr. Pimsleur earned a bachelor's degree at the City College of New York; he received a master's degree in psychological statistics and a Ph.D. in French, both from Columbia University.

He first taught French phonetics and phonemics at the University of California, Los Angeles. After leaving UCLA, Pimsleur went on to a faculty position at Ohio State University, where he taught French and foreign language education. At the time, the foreign language education program at OSU was the major doctoral program in the field in the United States. While there, he created and directed the Listening Center, one of the largest language laboratories in the United States. The center was developed in conjunction with Ohio Bell Telephone and allowed self-paced language study using a series of automated tapes and prompts that were delivered over the telephone.

Dr. Pimsleur, along with a number of renowned linguists and experts in the field of language teaching, was called to Washington, D.C., in 1962 for a discussion on what could be done to improve foreign-language teaching in the United States. Math and science were not the only areas that had been found wanting when the U.S. education system was examined in the wake of Sputnik and the Soviets winning the race to space.

Dr. Pimsleur proposed creating a self-study audio language program based on his own classroom methodology and his experience with students at the Listening Center. In order to be able to judge the effectiveness of his approach, he was asked to choose a language not familiar to most English speakers. He chose Greek, which also had the advantage of added difficulty because of a non-Latin alphabet.

Pimsleur and his wife, Beverly (who served as his researcher as he produced and recorded the course), went to Greece in March 1962. They returned in August of that year, and the first Pimsleur course, *Speak & Read Essential Greek: A Tapeway Program*, was self-published in March 1963. The subsequent languages undertaken by Dr. Pimsleur were French (1964), Spanish (1966), German (1967), and Twi (1971).

Later, Pimsleur was a professor of education and romance languages at the State University of New York in Albany, where he held dual professorships in education and French. He was a Fulbright lecturer at the Ruprecht Karls University of Heidelberg in 1968 and 1969 and a founding member of the American Council on the Teaching of Foreign Languages (ACTFL). He did research on the psychology of language learning, and in 1969 was the section head of psychology of second languages learning at the International Congress of Applied Linguistics.

His research focused on understanding the language acquisition process, especially the learning process of children, who speak a language without knowing its formal structure. The result of this research was the Pimsleur language learning system.

Through this research, he identified three factors that could be measured to calculate language aptitude: verbal intelligence, auditory ability, and motivation. He was one of the first foreign language educators to show an interest in students who have difficulty in learning a foreign language while doing well in other subjects.

After Dr. Pimsleur's death, the ACTFL-MLJ Paul Pimsleur Award for Research in Foreign Language Education was created and is awarded annually.

Foreword to the First Edition

The manuscript of this little book about foreign languages and how to learn them was placed in my hands by Paul Pimsleur's widow, Beverly Pimsleur, some three years after her husband's untimely death in Paris, where he was teaching at the Sorbonne.

She told me how very much Paul had wanted to see this book published and that she thought language students everywhere should have the opportunity to benefit from his insights and experiences as a master teacher. The pages of this book contain the essential advice that was at the very core of his own effective language teaching.

Some time later, after I had read the work and, I must confess, with great delight over both the content and the sparkling style, I called Beverly and told her that we wanted to publish it for two reasons: first, because the memory of her husband deserved this as a fitting tribute to his outstanding contributions to the field of language pedagogy; and second, because not to make it available would be a considerable loss to all language students, especially in the United States, where the study of foreign languages needs to be encouraged and developed so that North Americans can eventually take their place on the globe as citizens of the world!

This is clearly the place to mention the dream of Paul Pimsleur, to create a series of courses that would make easily accessible the major languages of the world to his fellow Americans in a way that would facilitate the removal of that black spot "the ugly Americans" from the lexicon of our neighbors on this ever-smaller globe.

In fact, Paul Pimsleur accomplished a large part of his dream with the creation of his *Speak and Read Essential Series,* cassette courses for French, Spanish, German, Greek, and one for the African language Twi. These cassette courses are probably the most effective tribute that could be made to the memory of this great language teacher, whose voice still sounds clear and vital as it speaks through the tapes to provide instruction, information, and encouragement to the un-counted numbers of everyday and not-so-everyday Americans who make the effort to expand their horizons and enjoy the culture and civilization of other countries.

Although *How to Learn a Foreign Language* is the posthumous publication of Paul Pimsleur, his dream, as exemplified in the *Speak and Read Essential Series,* remains very much alive and, I believe, will continue to provide effective language instruction for years to come. The voice of the master teacher still resonates and sparkles on the tape as he teaches to all who come and listen.

This publication, then, is for the language students of the world, in memory of Paul Pimsleur. Long may his voice be heard!

Charles A. S. Heinle, President
Heinle & Heinle Publishers, Inc.

The "Whys"
of Language Learning

A few years ago a prominent physician, head of neurophysiology at a medical school, struck up a conversation with me at a party. When he discovered that I was a language teacher, he grew eager to relate to me his bad experience with languages in school. His tone of voice made it plain that he had a long-standing negative recollection and wanted to get it off his mind.

"French was destroyed for me," he said, "by my junior high school teacher . . . who was actually a gym teacher substituting in French." He explained that the teacher had a very poor accent. He found this out when his parents helped him with his homework one day. They taught him to pronounce certain words that his teacher had completely mispronounced. From then on, he was obliged to mispronounce them deliberately in class, to avoid offending the teacher.

The physician went on to Cornell University. There he learned Russian, mastering it well enough to take advanced courses where only Russian was spoken. But even his success with Russian was not enough to offset his belief that he was poor at French—incapable of learning a language that he knew to be easier than Russian.

This sort of incident is not a rarity. Especially in well-to-do neighborhoods where families go abroad, many children pronounce the foreign language better than their teachers, and encounter difficulties in their classes when they might be enjoying a special sense of mastery.

This book is about foreign languages and how to learn them. However, as in the case of the aggrieved physician, so many people come to this subject traumatized by bad experiences in school that some common misconceptions must be laid to rest before we can even approach what for many people is a "loaded" topic.

The following statistics indicate the extent of harm done in high school language classes. Of all students who take a language in high school, half drop it after only one year. By the end of two years, nine out of ten have given up language study entirely. A very small percentage of U.S. high school students actually learn a foreign language well enough to read it comfortably or to speak it with any fluency. Most of the rest come away convinced that they cannot learn a foreign language.

People in many parts of the world speak several languages as a matter of course. In Africa, there are places where practically everyone speaks four or five languages daily.

How a person does with languages in grade or high school provides virtually no indication of how he might fare trying to learn them as an adult. But one must overcome powerful misgivings in many cases. How does one do this? And how does one master a language? Why would one want to learn a language? How long should it take? How should one go about it? These are the prime questions to which this book addresses itself.

1. Everyone Can Learn Another Language

Intelligence

According to reliable studies, only about 16 percent of what it takes to learn a foreign language is attributable to intelligence—at least as defined by IQ tests. IQ tests are largely made up of English vocabulary and mathematical reasoning questions, presented in various forms. Perhaps this explains why IQ correlates better with success in school than with success in life. Doing well in languages, like doing well at business, politics, or love, calls for more than the type of intelligence that makes you successful in school. It demands qualities like persuasiveness, sensitivity, gaiety, and perseverance, which IQ tests make no attempt to measure.

Musical Ability

Study after study have shown that, contrary to popular belief, musical ability accounts for only about 10 percent of what it takes to learn a language. While we can all think of people we have known who play the piano brilliantly and also learn foreign languages easily, a few moments' reflection will probably call to mind nearly as many opposite instances—people who are musical whizzes but know no foreign languages. The relationship between the two is far too slight to predict with any certainty that a musically apt person will do better at learning a language than someone with a poor ear for music.

Language Talent and You

One of the main reasons why people despair of studying a language is that it "makes them feel stupid." To the world, one is a competent adult, but to a language teacher one may sound like a babbling baby, forced to stammer out even the simplest ideas. At least this is how a great number of adult students report having felt.

In contrast with daily life, where we can usually avoid situations that embarrass us, in the classroom we are helpless in front of a teacher who can, by an ill-timed question, expose our ignorance. A ludicrous accent or a blatant mistake in grammar might identify us as incompetent.

When they fail to recognize this, teachers may misuse their power. The classroom, as anyone who has taught will verify, is a loaded game. The teacher is more than merely one of the players: he lays down the rules and also acts as the sole referee. For instance, it is within his power to humiliate a student for forgetting vocabulary words, when actually he himself may be to blame for not providing sufficient practice. Too easily, when the teacher becomes unreasonable in his demands, the student feels incompetent. He decides that the fault is with his own ability and gives up.

Still, you may say, there must be some people with so little talent for foreign languages that they would be well advised not to waste time trying to learn one. Perhaps this is so, but I for one do not believe it, and in any event it is extremely hard to tell in individual cases.

A young man in a French class I was teaching at UCLA was doing poorly and in danger of failing the course. I sent him to a good tutor, with whose help he managed to scrape through. I guess that, if I had reflected, I would have considered him an example of someone with no talent for languages.

I happened to run into the young man again a year or so later on a street in Athens. He had been living there for two months with a Greek family, and had already learned enough Greek to hold down a job. When we sat down at a sidewalk café to chat, he had the satisfaction of ordering for both of us, in fluent Greek. He had learned Greek but not French. The talent was in him, though he himself might not have believed it.

I have seen other incorrigible cases, like the Army sergeant who was sent back to school at age fifty to learn Cambodian. He did miserably and soon decided to retire from the Army rather than stay in the language school. This was too bad. The sergeant, like many supposed "no language talent" people, was probably as capable as most of learning a language if the circumstances had been right. If he had parachuted into a Cambodian village, he might have learned the language very quickly.

Discouragement, frustration, and fatigue produce a tremendous impulse to give up before one gets far enough for competence to bring its own reward. The best defense against this is to know before starting exactly what you want to accomplish and why.

Why Learn a Foreign Language?

It takes considerable effort to learn a foreign language, too much for people who vaguely hope to get a better job using such knowledge. English has become the worldwide language of business, and in firms where knowing a foreign language is a job requirement, most find it simpler to employ a foreign person than to train an American employee.

Many people want to learn a foreign language for reasons that are no less real for being "impractical." Such reasons are often deeply personal.

When I was in my early twenties, I took up Russian. I told my friends it was because Russian was becoming an important world language. However, my true reason, which I recognized later, was that I had hoped to find, in the language of my Slavic grandparents, a clue to my own occasional pessimism.

Similarly, courses in Greek, in Japanese, and in African languages are attended by many people seeking a deeper awareness of themselves and hoping to find it in the language of their ancestors.

Some people are interested in learning a foreign language simply because they cannot consider themselves as educated without it. Such a person might explain that motivation by saying, "It makes me feel like a whole person, a citizen of the world."

I think the best answer to "Why learn a foreign language?" is that it may make one's life richer. Not only after one knows it, but even during the learning. That languages take time to learn becomes a plus instead of a drawback when one considers how such a long-range commitment gives focus and continuity to a period of one's life. Viewed as a decision to fill a stretch of time with stimulating, purposeful activity, the undertaking of learning a foreign language can be a delightful voyage full of new expressions and ideas. One is glad to go slowly and savor the trip, especially when there are no judges to satisfy other than oneself.

2. When Is a Language Easy to Learn?

Contrary to what most people believe, pronunciation is not the hardest feature of a language to master. Nor is grammar.

A language—any language—has three distinct components: *pronunciation*, *grammar*, and *vocabulary*. A closer look at these components will reveal that the third is the most difficult to master.

Pronunciation

Human beings are limited in the speech sounds they can produce. For one thing, all of us have the same vocal apparatus—tongue, lips, vocal cords, and so on—which we use in roughly similar ways.

Then, too, sounds must remain distinct from one another; if there were too many, listeners might have trouble distinguishing them. Linguists tell us that no known language is composed of fewer sounds than Hawaiian, which has fifteen, or more than certain languages of the Caucasus, which have up to sixty. Most languages fall somewhere between these two extremes; English and French, for example, have thirty-one sounds.

Fortunately for the learner, in most languages fewer than half a dozen sounds are difficult to imitate. And within the first few weeks of study, this number typically dwindles to one or two.

One should always strive to achieve a native-like accent; this is part of the ambition to learn the language well. But we must concede that a person can thrive in a foreign country, converse freely, and even conduct business though his accent may be far from perfect.

Relatively speaking, pronunciation poses less of a learning challenge than grammar or vocabulary.

Grammar

People who have learned several foreign languages report that learning grammar becomes easier after having mastered the first two languages. Through knowing three languages, they discover that there are simple unifying principles underlying grammar's apparent complexity.

Languages exist so that human beings can communicate experience. Since all human beings share a common physiology and common basic needs, it is little wonder that all languages have certain features in common. English conveys the idea of going *into a room* by those three words, in that fixed order; Finnish conveys the same idea by a suffix, as if one were to say "roominto." The point is that both languages have a way of conveying the "into" idea.

Similarly, all languages have devices for conveying whether an action is presently going on (*she is dancing*) or is finished (*she danced*); for relating people and things to each other (*Jack's wife; our car*); for replacing a noun (*the woman*) by a pronoun (*she*).

Anthropologists working in the remotest corners of the world have been amazed to discover that all people, however "primitive" they may appear from our point of view, possess a language whose grammar is systematic, internally consistent, and well adapted to their life needs. There is no such thing as a primitive grammar.

An experienced language learner is one who knows approximately what to expect when he confronts the grammar of a new language. He knows that he will encounter both good and bad surprises. If he decides to study Finnish, for example, he will be delighted to find it has a very simple number system. (A friend of mine once learned the Finnish numbers from zero to infinity during a two-hour flight to Helsinki.) He will be dismayed to find it has a formidable variety of word-endings. But having learned other languages, he will be psychologically ready both to enjoy learning the numbers and to struggle with the word-endings. He has seen this sort of thing before and knows it can be mastered.

In learning grammar, we are buoyed up in moments of discouragement by knowing that the task is limited. If you take any language textbook and add up the space occupied by rules of grammar (distinct from exercises, readings, and other content), you will find it surprisingly compact. The basic grammar of a language can generally be explained, with copious examples, in fewer than one hundred pages.

This is not to suggest that the way to learn grammar is to memorize those one hundred pages. Some people do go about swallowing grammar whole that way, but for most of us there are more palatable methods. Whatever the method, however, one is bound to hit some snags along the way. The knowledge that there is only so much grammar, and no more, can help rekindle a person's courage when a tough point of grammar makes the language seem impossible to master.

Vocabulary

Words, words, words. It takes about fifteen hundred of them for a "basic" command of a language and perhaps five thousand to be really fluent. This is a challenge to anyone's learning ability, however gifted he may be. However, if a person can recognize some foreign words from his own language, or from a third language that he knows, the task will obviously be much simpler.

As a general rule, languages closely related to one's own are easiest to learn, for one may find helpful similarities in pronunciation, one is likely to find them in grammar, and one is virtually sure to find them in vocabulary.

As native speakers of English, Americans are in a favorable position to learn foreign languages, for English is related to *two* important language families. We enjoy a head start whether we are learning a *Romance* language (French, Spanish, Italian, Portuguese, Romanian, and Catalan) or a *Teutonic* language (German, Dutch, Flemish, Afrikaans, Norwegian, Danish, Swedish, and Icelandic).

English is a Teutonic language. The early settlers of England were German-speaking tribes whose dialect gradually developed into a separate language. The affinities between German and English are still quite evident today.

French and English, on the other hand, were never one language. The Normans conquered England in 1066 and occupied it for some two hundred years, during which time the upper classes spoke only French, while the lower classes continued speaking English. In the years following the Norman conquest, about ten thousand French words entered the English language. Some 75 percent of them are still in common use.

An American can recognize many French words easily—and therefore learn them easily. The point is worth demonstrating, so I have listed on the following page fifty words taken at random from a French dictionary. Doing a column at a time, try to guess their meaning. Some are completely obvious, others less so. Write down what you think each one means, then compare your answers with those given on page 101, giving yourself credit if you are even approximately correct. When you have done all five columns, calculate your total score. (If you know French, you may want to ask someone to try this who does not.)

The average American who knows no French can guess fifteen to seventeen of these words correctly—about 30 percent. Anyone who has ever studied French, even long ago, can probably recognize 40 or even 50 percent.

1	2	3	4	5
frère	cours	bonheur	existence	lendemain
jardin	plan	garde	détail	volonté
sentiment	rôle	valeur	colère	marche
scène	malheur	habitude	salon	madame
situation	envie	sang	journal	foule
arbre	endroit	couleur	fleur	garçon
impression	roi	sujet	bouche	geste
larme	franc	titre	rapport	société
goût	champ	soin	foi	salle
loi	importance	faute	groupe	joie
Score____	Score____	Score____	Score____	Score____
Total Score____				

Approximately the same demonstration could be made for Spanish, Italian, or German. The point is that an American learning any of these languages already "knows" every third or fourth word, which reduces the task of learning vocabulary considerably.

Significantly, this advantage actually grows with time. At first one must learn the little words that glue the language together (I, you; is, are; before, after); as a rule, these do not resemble English. Later on, however, one focuses on "content" words—mainly nouns, verbs, and adjectives—and has the pleasure of recognizing many of these quite readily.

Which Are the "Easy" and "Hard" Languages?

No school in America is more experienced at teaching foreign languages to adults than the Foreign Service Institute of the U.S. Department of State. Located in Arlington, Virginia, the FSI has been training diplomats and other government personnel for service overseas for more than twenty-five years.

Here is how the FSI rates the languages they teach, based on the difficulty their students have had over the years in mastering them. Group 1 is "easiest," Group 4 the "hardest."

Group 1	*Group 2*	*Group 3*	*Group 4*
French	Bulgarian	Amharic	Arabic
German	Burmese	Cambodian	Chinese
Indonesian	Greek	Czech	Japanese
Italian	Hindi	Finnish	Korean
Portuguese	Persian	Hebrew	
Romanian	Urdu	Hungarian	
Spanish		Lao	
Swahili		Polish	
		Russian	
		Serbo-Croatian	
		Thai	
		Turkish	
		Vietnamese	

As expected, the languages closest to English are all on the "easy" list. Somewhat surprisingly, however, two other languages are also on that list: Indonesian (Malay) and Swahili. Though unrelated to English, they have proven fairly easy for Americans to learn, and any reader contemplating a trip to an area where one of these is spoken should not hesitate to study the language before he goes. He is likely to find it no more difficult than, say, a language he took in high school, and knowing even a little of it will make an enormous difference in his trip.

3. How Long Does It Take to Learn a Language?

Some people would be very glad if they could say even a few phrases in a foreign language with a passable accent. Others mainly want to read great works of literature. Still others may aspire to speak and write another language as fluently as their mother tongue.

Before travel abroad became common, foreign languages were associated in this country with educated people and immigrants. The former were often interested only in reading and writing a particular language, while the latter could speak their native language but had little occasion to read or write it after coming to America. Some educated people resembled the upper-class British gentlemen of the nineteenth century who typically "knew" French but were disinclined to imitate the "peculiar" sounds a Frenchman makes when speaking.

In today's world, many people who study a foreign language chiefly desire to speak it. It is important, therefore, to estimate how well a person can expect to speak a language after studying it for a certain number of hours—and conversely, how many hours it may take him to reach the fluency he has in mind. Several estimates will follow on how long it takes to achieve various sorts of mastery, based on FSI data and my own research.

The FSI Rating Scale

Many U.S. government agencies use the FSI Absolute Language Proficiency Ratings to measure a prospective employee's ability to use a foreign language in his work. Once employed, he periodically undergoes the same type of rating as a basis for promotion.

The person to be rated is interviewed by one or more trained testers, who are always native speakers. They converse with him for ten to twenty minutes, probing his command of pronunciation, grammar, and vocabulary. Then they pool their judgments to assign him a rating. The lowest rating is 1, the highest 5, and any rating can be modified by a plus or minus.

Each rating designates a particular degree of mastery of the language for business and social purposes:

1. *Elementary proficiency.* The person is able to satisfy routine travel needs and minimum courtesy requirements.
2. *Limited working proficiency.* The person is able to satisfy routine social demands and limited work requirements.
3. *Minimum professional proficiency.* The person can speak the language with sufficient structural accuracy and vocabulary to participate effectively in most formal and informal conversations on practical, social, and professional topics.
4. *Full professional proficiency.* The person uses the language fluently and accurately on all levels normally pertinent to professional needs.
5. *Native or bilingual proficiency.* The person has speaking proficiency equivalent to that of an educated native speaker.

How long, one wonders, does it take a person to achieve the minimum 1, and how much longer after that to reach a 2 or 3?

FSI researchers studied the performance of all their students during a three-year period, noting the ratings they received after various periods of training. Table 1 shows the results for the "easy" languages, and for the "hard" languages.

In reality, these time estimates are a little lower than they at first appear; holidays and other lost time reduce them by about 10 percent. Nevertheless, the meaning is clear. If you are a language learner of average ability, and you undertake an "easy" language, it will probably take you about 220 hours to get to the first level of mastery in speaking it, and double that to get to Level 2. If you are slower than average at learning languages, allow 50 percent more time; if faster, 50 percent less.

Table 1. Learning Rates for "Easy" and "Hard" Languages

"Easy" Languages		"Hard" Languages	
Ratings of FSI students speaking a Group 1 language after specified periods of training.		Ratings of FSI students speaking Group 2-4 language after specified periods of training.	
Training Period	*Proficiency Rating*	*Training Period*	*Proficiency Rating*
8 weeks (240 hours)	1/1+	12 weeks (360 hours)	1/1+
16 weeks (480 hours)	2	24 weeks (720 hours)	1+/2
24 weeks (720 hours)	2+	44 weeks (1320 hours)	2/2+/3

These figures are based on a particular type of instruction: the FSI intensive course where one studies a language for six hours a day, five days a week, in a class of no more than ten students, led by an experienced linguist and well-trained native drillmaster. The school is a language learning paradise, the students are highly motivated, and optimum results are achieved. Yet these estimates are reasonably valid for people who, like most of us, have no choice but to attend a conventional course that meets forty-five minutes a day or a couple of evenings a week.

Human attention is limited. No one can absorb knowledge steadily for six hours a day, week after week; some of the time in intensive courses is necessarily "wasted" in relaxing, clearing one's mind, or plain daydreaming. Moreover, things that seem confusing one day sometimes clear up by the next, after they have settled into place in one's mind. This "incubation" factor favors a non-intensive learning schedule. In short, it is not certain that people who spread their language learning over a longer period necessarily require more total hours than those who concentrate. They may even require fewer.

The overriding message is that anyone can learn a foreign language, but some people are quicker at it than others. Still, language learning is a serious commitment, and if one's aim is to speak it comfortably (say, 2+ on the FSI scale), this is likely to take the equivalent of six months of full-time study.

However, fluency in speaking is not everyone's chief objective. An alternative objective, perhaps less demanding, may correspond to your needs and desires.

Alternative Goals

Not everyone is interested in the types of objectives set by the FSI. Some people want to speak a language just well enough to get along in a foreign country; others may want mainly to read it. Moreover, the instruction the average person is likely to find available will probably not resemble that at the FSI. Another set of estimates may be required for the average person, given average instruction.

THE "COURTESY AND NECESSITY" SPEAKING LEVEL. You may want to speak the language just well enough to exchange politenesses with people you meet, order food and drink, and ask for a doctor if you need one. Don't undervalue even this; it is a degree of mastery that can transform a person from an "ugly American" into one who is obviously attempting to meet others halfway. It is certain to make any trip you take more rewarding.

Evidence from people who have used my programmed language courses shows that this type of mastery can be achieved in less than sixty hours, which comes to only an hour a day for two to three months—an excellent return for a limited effort.

READING ONLY. If you set out learning to read the foreign language, and forgo the effort to speak or write it, then in 100 to 150 hours you will be able to read material related to your line of work with ease. This amounts to six hours per week for four to six months—again, a useful skill one can acquire at a modest price in time. However, you should not expect your reading skill to help you if you later decide to learn to speak. Speaking and reading are two very different activities, and though reading builds vocabulary, it may actually damage pronunciation.

BALANCED COMPETENCE. It is entirely possible, by taking a foreign language course sequence in a college "extension" division or at the YMCA, to become able to read with ease, understand the gist of what you hear, and write a satisfactory business or personal letter. At the rate of six hours per week—three of class and three of homework—a person of average aptitude can acquire a fair mastery in two years' time. He should not expect, however, to be completely fluent in speaking, nor to understand everything he hears.

EDUCATED MASTERY. If your objective is to master the language fully in speech and writing, then you may have to devote at least a year and a half, most of it spent in the foreign country, to reaching this objective. A good plan would be to study the language for three to six months at home, and then go to the foreign country for at least a year, during which time you must speak only the foreign language. At the end of this time, you would understand most people and even television and movies, read almost any written matter without a dictionary, and perhaps write with a modicum of style. Adults who go abroad to live find that after several months of getting adjusted to speaking and understanding in everyday situations, they can then begin to penetrate the language and participate in the life of the country.

Some people are dismayed by time estimates that run to hundreds of hours. They feel that this is more time than they are willing to commit. They should reflect on the fact that one year from today they will be one year older whether they undertake this learning task or not. The only question is whether, on that day, they are going to be well along toward mastering the language they have dreamed of knowing, or whether it will still be only a dream.

4. Which Language Should You Select?

When actress Ingrid Bergman, who knew five languages, was asked which she preferred, she replied: "English for acting, Italian for romance, French for diplomacy, German for philosophy ... and Swedish for secrecy, because so few people know it."

Which language should *you* take up? French sounds pretty. But Mexico is closer. Or would Italian be easier?

If you have very strong motives for learning some particular language, you may want to skip the following discussion of the hard and easy points of various languages, for a strong desire to learn can override all other considerations. Any language is learnable provided your will to learn it is strong enough to keep you going when tedium sets in.

If you are still reading, you apparently have not yet fixed on a choice. In all likelihood, you are looking for a language to study that will be useful and agreeable for travel and social contacts, and perhaps for business as well. The best way to help you choose is to describe the most popular languages so you will know what to expect if you elect to study one of them.

French

The tough part may be the pronunciation. French has fourteen vowel sounds, none of them quite the same as in English, and an ill-fitting writing system where words don't necessarily look the way they sound.

Vocabulary, on the other hand, is easier in French than in any other language, due to the overlap with English.

The grammar is a little more difficult than in Spanish, though not nearly so difficult as in German or Russian.

The payoff for learning French is great: a rich literature to read, endless possibilities for the tourist who knows the language, and worldwide social prestige.

Verdict: if you are reasonably good at telling dialect jokes and imitating foreign accents, then French pronunciation should hold no terror for you. But if you have a poor ear, or get mixed up easily in spelling, or cannot tolerate "illogical" grammar, then maybe you had better pick a language farther down the list.

German

With only a few sounds that are different from English, German is an easy language to pronounce. It is also easy to "get along" in German on the damn-the-grammar basis, for the Germans are nice about trying to understand what you say, no matter how you massacre their language.

German vocabulary seems hard at first, but becomes easier when you reach the plateau where word-roots begin to reappear. You soon find yourself able to correctly guess the meaning of words you have never seen or heard before.

The grammar of German is more difficult than that of the Romance languages—though less than that of Russian—so don't expect to progress from "pidgin" to proper German without serious study.

Verdict: if you don't mind learning grammar as long is it is orderly, then German may be for you. The effort of learning it is amply rewarded by the countries you can visit (Switzerland and Austria as well as Germany) and the many books, plays, and operas you can enjoy when you know it.

Italian

The "language of love" is only moderately difficult. It has few troublesome sounds, a regular spelling system, and grammar of only average difficulty. The payoff is good, though only in one country, Italy, where you can enjoy art, opera, food, sunshine, and lively people.

Verdict: if you are strongly attracted to Italian, go ahead and learn it; it is easier for Americans than most other languages. You may have more trouble, though, finding a good Italian course than one in French, Spanish, or German.

Spanish

The pronunciation of Spanish is a little harder than Italian or German, but not so hard as that of French. Spelling is very regular. Vocabulary is almost as easy to guess at as in French. Grammar is made easier by the regularity of verbs. The payoff in business and cultural value is considerable, since Spanish is spoken by so many people in so many places.

Verdict: if you wish to learn a language that can be used in a variety of countries in both hemispheres, then take Spanish because it is fairly easy and there are many ways to put it to use as you are learning.

Russian

People often are frightened of the Russian (Cyrillic) alphabet, which turns out in practice to be easy to master. However, other features of the language—one or two difficult sounds, elaborate grammar rules, and vocabulary that cannot be guessed at—make Russian harder for Americans than the languages mentioned so far. Examine your motive before you begin: is it strong enough to carry you through a long period of study? Remember also that you cannot expect to spend a great deal of time as a tourist in the Soviet Union, and that Russian is not widely spoken in areas where Americans may reside.

Verdict: Russian is difficult but rewarding, provided you have a compelling purpose for learning it.

Other Languages

These five languages—French, German, Italian, Spanish, and Russian—account for 95 percent of all foreign language instruction in the United States ... which merely proves that our view of the world is lopsided and badly out of date. We favor a few prestigious European languages but ignore languages like Japanese, Arabic, and Hindi that are spoken by tens or even hundreds of millions of people who boast cultural heritages that rival those of any European country.

There are estimated to be some three thousand to five thousand languages in the world. The top twelve (see Table 2 on the following page) comprise 65 percent of the world's population. However, there are over a hundred other languages spoken by at least a million people apiece. The path of real adventure for you may lie in studying a language outside the common five. If you are open to an undertaking that could change your life, then pick an area of the world that fascinates you and commit yourself to studying its politics, its economics, its history, its people, and at least one of its languages. Browse among the languages listed by geographic region in the appendix to this book entitled "Languages of the World." See which are spoken in a part of the world that attracts you. Then reflect on the business opportunities, the leisure-time activities, the retirement possibilities, or even the new career that you might find in committing yourself to a plan of "language and area" studies.

Table 2. The Twelve Most Widely Spoken Languages*

Language	No. of Users (in Millions)*
1. Mandarin Chinese	820
2. English	450†
3. Russian	270
4. Spanish	260
5. Hindi‡	165
6. Arabic	160
7. Portuguese	132
8. Bengali	130
9. German	120
10. Japanese	115
11. Indonesian-Malay	85
12. French	82

* As of 1980. All figures have to be rather rough estimates, since there are no generally reliable sources for such statistics.

† Conrad and Fishman in *The Spread of English* (1977, p. 6) estimate 600 million; this must extend to a rather rudimentary ability to use the language. (In J.A. Fishman, R.L. Cooper, and A.W. Conrad, Rowley, Mass.: Newbury House, 1977.)

‡ As spoken by ordinary villagers, Hindi and Urdu are nearly indistinguishable. The more formal the style, the more they diverge, because of Persian influence on Urdu and Sanskrit influence on Hindi. The writing systems for the two are totally different. The combined total for Hindi-Urdu is at least 217 million.

5. Learning the "Tricks of the Trade"

The Burton Story

Sir Richard Burton—not the actor but the great nineteenth century British adventurer who penetrated the forbidden sacred cities of Islam, discovered Lake Tanganyika, explored the Amazon, and shocked Victorian England with his detailed reports on sex practices in distant lands—*that* Richard Burton was also one of the great linguists of his time. A distinguished translator from Hindi, Portuguese, Arabic (*The Arabian Nights*) and several other languages, he was said to be able to pass for a native in twenty-nine languages, and to have developed a technique for learning a new language in two months' time. Burton described this technique in his memoirs:

I got a simple grammar and vocabulary, marked out the forms and words that I knew were absolutely necessary, and learnt them by heart by carrying them in my pocket and looking over them at spare moments during the day. I never worked for more than a quarter of an hour at a time, for after that the brain lost its freshness. After learning some three hundred words, easily done in a week, I stumbled through some easy workbook (one of the Gospels is the most come-atable), and underlined every word that I wished to recollect, in order to read over my pencillings at least once a day. Having finished my volume, I then carefully worked up the grammar minutiae, and I then chose some other book whose subject most interested me. The neck of the language was now broken, and progress was rapid. If I came across a new sound like the Arabic *Ghayn,* I trained my tongue to it by repeating it so many thousand times a day. When I read, I invariably read out loud, so that the ear might aid memory. I was delighted with the most difficult characters, Chinese and Cuneiform, because I felt that they impressed themselves more strongly upon the eye than the eternal Roman letters.... Whenever I conversed with anybody in a language that I was learning, I took the trouble to repeat their words inaudibly after them, and so to learn the trick of pronunciation and emphasis.

Burton's readiness to admit his stumbling and his short attention span brings him closer to us and makes us want to sort out what is illusory and what is real in the Burton legend.

Passing for a Native in Twenty-nine Languages

Don't be misled by reputations. Perhaps Burton *was* an utter master of all of his twenty-nine languages. But reputations are often overdone. I myself have a reputation for knowing a great number of languages, many more than I actually know.

Once, when a class had been pestering me to tell them how many languages I knew, I walked over to a Swedish exchange student in the class and held this conversation with her in Swedish.

    I: Are you Swedish?
    She: Yes, I am.
    I: What part of Sweden are you from?
    She: I'm from Linköping.

> I: I don't know it, where is it?
> She: (long answer about the location of the town)
> I: How long have you been in America?
> She: Since . . . (two-sentence answer)
> I: Thank you very much. Good-bye.

Our conversation lasted for about three minutes. Then I asked her in English whether she had readily understood my Swedish; she said she had. I asked the class whether, in their judgment, I was entitled to claim that I knew Swedish. They replied warmly that surely I could add Swedish to my list of languages . . . and were disappointed when I told them that I hardly knew Swedish at all and would consider myself fraudulent to maintain that I did.

My part in the conversation consisted merely of a few stock phrases, and some questions to keep the other person talking. Actually, my questions bore no relation to her answers, because I did not understand her. I was prepared to ask the same set of questions regardless of what she said.

The amount of Swedish I used in that "conversation" can be taught to anyone at all in an hour.

Burton himself was well aware of the difference between mastering a language and merely being able to say "please" and "thank you" in it. He never claimed for himself even a small part of what his idolators claimed for him.

Learning a Language in Two Months' Time

Stories go around about people, supposedly geniuses at languages, who cram great learning into short intervals. I am assuming my readers do not have time for this, even if they have the inclination. Even Burton probably spent just as many total hours as anyone else, only concentrating it in a short span of time.

If a person spent forty hours per week for two months learning a language, that totals about 350 hours—approximately the same amount of time the Foreign Service Institute estimates that it takes to attain "elementary proficiency," and the same amount of time a college student spends in three semesters of language study.

What we want to get out of the Burton experience is not how amazing he was, but what he *did*—what techniques he employed that other people might profitably imitate.

"I Never Worked for More Than a Quarter of an Hour at a Time . . ."

This statement by Burton is heartwarming.

Many people are discouraged about their lack of concentration. We often hear such statements as, "I can't fix my mind on anything anymore," or "I don't read serious books anymore; I just can't." In all probability, the people speaking expect too much of themselves, and then become discouraged when they cannot live up to their self-imposed expectations.

Like Burton, many people work better in short, concentrated spurts. If so, then that is the way they should study. Three spurts of twenty minutes each may add up to more than an hour in results achieved. The person who sits down to study for an hour often wastes a good part of it in sharpening pencils, getting a drink of water, and otherwise dawdling. The spurter tends to get the most out of his limited study time.

There are good and bad times to study, and people often fail to take advantage of the good ones. Early in the morning: by rising fifteen minutes earlier, you can read a page of Russian a day. At lunchtime: you could practice Italian for fifteen minutes rather than chatting with office-mates. Before dinner: a session with your vocabulary cards may help pass the time, and no rule forbids learning a language with a martini in your hand; in fact, it may lower your inhibitions.

I knew a man who used his shaving time to learn Chinese. He posted a few Chinese characters on his mirror every morning and looked at them while shaving. It cost him a nick or two, but within a few months he had learned five hundred Chinese characters solely while shaving.

6. Organic Learning

When you take a language in high school or college, you probably learn "conjugation" lists looking something like this:

I give
you give
he, she, it gives
we give
you give
they give

You may not be in school now, and there is no reason not to learn things in the order that strikes your fancy, rather than the order in which grammarians put them in. If you let the "need to know" be your guide, studying will retain its freshness longer.

You might learn the verb "to give," for example, by first learning the simple phrase "give me ..." You would practice it by saying things like, "Give me a scotch," "Give me your phone number," and so on. Soon this command form will become automatic. By then you may have begun to wonder how to say, *"Don't give me ..."* ("Don't give me red wine, give me white wine"). Then it is time to learn negative commands.

Later still, you will wonder how to say, "Give *her* . . . ," referring to another person. And still later, you'll want to say, "You *didn't* give me . . . ," a negative in the past tense.

Meanwhile, you will be working along on other fronts, picking up vocabulary, improving your pronunciation, practicing other grammar features. Your progress will come about in a natural way—*organically*.

In any growing organism, the parts develop in intimate interrelation to each other. Frank Lloyd Wright wrote in his *Autobiography*, "Perfect co-relation is the first principle of growth. Integration, or even the very word 'organic' itself, means that nothing is of value except as it is naturally related to the whole in the direction of some living purpose."

The common teaching method that obliges students to learn one complete verb conjugation at a time, even though they do not have the vocabulary and grammar to put that verb to work, is a monstrosity— as if a newly planted tree were suddenly to sprout one huge leaf instead of twigs and branches.

Moreover, it is a perfect prescription for tedium. Seeing no immediate use to which his hard-won knowledge can be put, a student must be exceptionally self-motivated to resist the desire to quit. In fact, statistics show that an overwhelming majority of language students do quit at the earliest possible moment.

Now that you are in charge of your own learning, the hobgoblin of completeness for its own sake need not dominate your work. Whether you tackle a language on your own, or prefer the regularity and discipline of a course, you are free to pick and choose. If certain vocabulary words or certain points of grammar do not mean anything to you right now, you can let them go, knowing you can pick them up at a later time.

Let the "living purpose" for which you undertook the language be your guide in how to learn it.

You can pick and choose among teachers, too. A good teacher will hold your interest longer, helping you to stick it out when learning becomes difficult. Search until you find one. You may have to try out several teachers before you find the especially gifted one you are seeking, but the effort will be worth your while.

How to Recognize a Good Teacher

I want to compare the first day of class in two different language classes that I visited at a major university.

Teacher A walked into his Japanese class on the first day, greeted his students, and began describing the sounds of Japanese. He contrasted them with the English sounds, using a number of technical terms like "voiceless" and "semi-vowel," which most of his students did not understand. But he went right on. Japanese, he explained, is a "syllable-timed" language; the typical syllable is CV (consonant + vowel); there are a total of 105 possible syllables. His prepared lecture took up the entire class hour.

On the first day of teacher B's Swahili class, he said hello to his students in English and then conducted the entire class in Swahili. He taught them to stand up when he said "stand" in Swahili, and to sit down when he said "sit." Then, pantomiming the arrival of a visitor at an African home, he taught the class to hold this conversation:

Visitor: (knocks) Anyone home?
   Host: Who's there?
Visitor: It's ... (name).
   Host: Come in, come in.
Visitor: (enters) Hello, how are you?
   Host: Fine, thank you. And you?
Visitor: Very well, thank you.
   Host: Please sit down.
Visitor: Thank you. (sits down)

When Teacher A's class ended, his students were apprehensive. They had not understood all the phonetic terms, and felt they could not possibly master 105 syllables. The only word of useful Japanese they had heard during that hour was the greeting of the teacher when he entered.

Teacher B's Swahili students were also a little apprehensive. They had met pronunciation difficulties and they were sure they could not remember everything they had learned. But they were exhilarated, too. They had spoken Swahili, learned useful greetings, and gotten good-natured fun out of each other's confusion. An *espirit de corps* had been established, and while it was clear that learning Swahili was going to be challenging, they were certainly eager for more.

I believe it is fair to ask, at the end of a language lesson, be it the first or the fiftieth, "What did I learn today that would help me if I left immediately for the foreign country?" If Class A and Class B had flown to their respective countries right after that first lesson, the Swahili students would have deplaned with a few words of greeting on their lips, while the Japanese students would have known no more Japanese than if the lesson had never taken place.

There are more Teacher A's than Teacher B's, and it is not always easy to tell them apart, so I would like to list some specifics of teacher behavior that may help you to recognize a good teacher.

TEACHER-TALK VERSUS STUDENT-TALK. Knowing that it takes a lot of practice to learn a foreign language, a good language teacher keeps the clock constantly in mind. Curbing his own tendency to expound, he disciplines himself to talk very little while getting his students to talk a lot. One way to judge a teacher is to calculate the ratio of teacher-talk to student-talk. With a good teacher, it will be heavily in favor of student-talk.

ENGLISH VERSUS FOREIGN LANGUAGE. How much time does the class spend using English when they could be using the foreign language? A good teacher teaches his class, early in the course, to understand all the repetitive pieces of classroom business: "open your books," "go to the board," "listen carefully," "repeat after me," "say it once more." All that and more can be done in the foreign language soon after the course begins. As a general rule, no more than five minutes of a class ought to be spent talking English—just enough to get a tough grammar point across or give an important assignment. The rest can and should be spent in the foreign language.

KEEPING GRAMMAR EXPLANATIONS SHORT. Grammar is best learned by using it, not by talking about it. A teacher should direct his efforts, not into preparing elaborate explanations, but into devising clever drills that get students to use grammar almost without realizing it. Experience shows that there is not a single point of grammar in an elementary course that cannot be explained in four minutes or less. If a teacher goes on longer than that, he is stealing time from the class's real need: practice, practice, practice.

AVOIDING PRIVATE DISCUSSIONS. A good teacher does not hold lengthy discussions with individual students during class. If an explanation is requested that is not appropriate for the whole class to hear, the teacher should either offer to discuss it after class or ask the student to hold his question until a later time when the point will become clear. An efficient teacher keeps the clock in mind and resumes the class without delay. No private discussions during class time, please.

ASKING A QUESTION. The question-and-answer technique is absolutely basic to language teaching, but a poorly trained teacher may mishandle it. He may allow one or two "pushy" students to monopolize the questions. Or he may "telegraph" his questions by indicating in advance which student is going to be called on; the others then "tune out." A good teacher directs all questions to the entire class, and does not call on anyone until all have had a moment to think of an answer. Then, if the first student called on does not have the answer ready, the teacher moves on quickly to someone else. Moving rapidly from student to student, he gives everyone a fair chance, increases the class's alertness, and provides more practice for each student. This technique also tends to suppress "eager beavers."

Teachers are paid professionals. They should be judged, at least in part, the cost-accounting way: by output per unit of time. A student is entitled to ask whether the hours he spends in the language class are giving him a fair return in usable language skills.

7. The Words and the Music

Every language has its own music, its rise and fall, its smoothness or choppiness. One can listen for these alone, with all meaning tuned out, like listening to a hubbub of voices in a crowded room, perceiving only the melody, not the words.

Our three-year-old son's first exposure to German came when we took him to Austria and he began to play with neighborhood children. He said nothing at first, just listened. Then he gradually developed a gibberish language of his own. The "words" were a meaningless babble, but they contained German sounds like *ch* and *ü* and the guttural *r*, and had the same singsong intonation as the local children. His conversations with them were hilarious. They talked to him in German, and he answered in fluent gibberish, with an authentic Tyrolean accent. He claimed he was "talking German," and was amazed when the others failed to understand him.

The music of a language, its *intonation*, strikes you even when you cannot comprehend a single word. It can also be the first thing you learn. Even before enrolling in a course, you can absorb the new accent by listening to someone speak the language and imitating the sounds he makes. Use nonsense syllables as in singing, "Tum-de-dum-dum."

Better still, imitate the way the foreign person speaks English. A foreign accent is merely the transfer of speech habits from one language to another, and one can infer a good deal about French, for example, from the way a Frenchman talks English.

Speech habits, acquired during one's formative years, are deeply ingrained. Very few people past adolescence are capable of giving theirs up in favor of a new set, hence very few people learn to speak a foreign language like a native. But when you set out to learn a new language, you want to give yourself every chance to master it utterly. One way to begin is by imitating, in English, the accent of the language you have chosen. It is like learning the music of a song first, so you can later concentrate completely on the words.

Trust Your Ear

One March afternoon in 1772, James Boswell was visiting his friend Dr. Samuel Johnson, author of a famous English dictionary, at his home in the Fleet Street section of London. They were discussing another dictionary that had recently appeared.

Boswell: It may be of use, sir, to have a dictionary to ascertain the pronunciation.

Johnson: Why, sir, my dictionary shows the accents of words if you can but remember them.

Boswell: But, sir, we want marks to ascertain the pronunciation of the vowels. Sheridan, I believe, has finished such a work.

Johnson: Why, sir, will you consider how much easier it is to learn a language by the ear than by any marks. Sheridan's dictionary may do very well. But you cannot always carry it about with you; and when you want the word, you have not the dictionary. It is like a man who has a sword that will not draw. It is an admirable sword, to be sure. But while your enemy is cutting your throat, you cannot draw this sword.

I once had a similar experience when I paid a visit to a business executive in Chicago. He was the president of a large publishing house, and was interested in having me demonstrate a self-teaching method I had recently devised in Greece. It is pertinent to explain that the method was (and still is) fully oral: the person taking the lessons holds simulated conversations with native Greeks, guided by an American teacher, all recorded on cassettes.

I set the executive up with a recorder, got him started on Lesson One, and left the room. When I returned at the end of the half-hour lesson, I found that, contrary to my instructions, he had taken out an envelope and jotted down all the Greek words in the lesson. He held it up proudly as I entered. "I think I got them all," he said.

I have watched dozens of people take that same lesson, and they virtually always emerge able to say a number of Greek phrases fluently. This man, however, ended up with a list of words on the back of an envelope. The Greek was in his pocket, but not in his mind; he had a sword that would not draw.

Like many people, this important executive lacked faith in the spoken word. He trusted only what he could see written down.

A person studying a language has got to trust the spoken word, insubstantial and evanescent though it is. He must have faith that sounds, although invisible, have a substance and a character of their own. He must accept as his objective to learn them, the sounds, rather than their written representation. And when there is a conflict, when a word does not look the way it sounds, then it is the sound he must believe in and cling to.

Many people, even many teachers, fall prey to the fallacy that the written form of a language is the language itself. Such teachers then make the error of teaching from the written to the spoken language, instead of vice versa. Pierre Delattre, a respected authority on languages and language teaching, explains why this is wrong.

It appears that the basic error in language teaching methods is one of *order*. We put the cart before the horse. *We use the eye before we use the ear; we take up writing before we take up speaking; we teach reading before we teach pronouncing; we study the rules before we study the examples; we concentrate on quantity before we concentrate on quality.* In all this, our error is that we go against the facts of language. A language is first of all "speech"—a system of sounds transmitted directly from mouth to ear and produced by automatic reactions of the speech organs. The functioning of those automatic reactions depends on the linguistic habits of the speaker, and it is the acquisition of those habits that must come first.

Language, as Delattre says, is above all speech, not writing: a language that is not spoken is called "dead." If you will trust your ear, you are almost certain to speak with a good accent. Conversely, if you trust your eye alone, your accent may be a poor one.

Short-Range Objectives
Learning a foreign language is like filling a bucket from a slow-running tap. If you keep looking in to see if it is full, you grow more and more impatient. You may finally kick it over and walk away. But if the bucket has notches that show when it is one-quarter full, one-third full, and so on, then you can take pleasure in watching the water rise from notch to notch. The filling time is the same, but the psychological effect is different.

In learning a language, the long-range purpose—to master the foreign tongue—often appears unattainable. One must have short-range goals as well.

Suppose you have decided to study Spanish. Some of your short-range goals might be: to master the present tense of certain verbs; to pronounce the trilled *r*; to read your first magazine article in Spanish;

to order food from a Spanish menu. These goals can be reached with a limited effort, and you can take delight in reaching them.

The teacher's function is to set day-to-day goals, encouraging his students to concentrate, not on the distant objective of total fluency, but on taking one more step. A good teacher will break the language down into manageable tasks, help you to accomplish them, and reward you when you do. It is not so much his knowledge that counts; one can find that in a book or record. His skill in fashioning a long chain of learning into viable, satisfying links is what keeps his students moving along when they might otherwise be tempted to quit.

The "Hows"
of Language Learning

Often, teachers assign new material to be learned as "homework": "Do the next three pages at home and we'll go over them tomorrow." As a teaching strategy, this is cockeyed, for it leaves the student on his own just when he most needs help. Alone with the new vocabulary or the new points of grammar, he is free to make mistakes and learn wrong forms to his heart's content. They must be unlearned later.

Skilled teachers—there are many of them and I have a great fondness for them even though, for purposes of this book, I have pointed out numerous classroom errors—skilled teachers, I say, prefer to present new material themselves, in class, so they can provide instant correction during the first few crucial stages of learning.

Still, regardless of how skilled a teacher he has been fortunate enough to find, the language student will generally have to supplement the classwork at home. What follows is a set of techniques and principles, gleaned from experienced language learners, for studying foreign languages. The list is not exhaustive; every person must develop his own techniques to suit his capacities and learning styles. But you are likely to find these techniques effective whether you are taking a language in school or studying one on your own.

8. How to Practice Pronunciation

Danny Kaye in his comedy routines used to rattle off a chain of sounds with a foreign accent and foreign gestures. The audience was convinced he was talking French when he was actually saying only nonsense syllables, pronounced with a heavy French accent. He could do this in several languages.

The music of a foreign language is different from the words. If you know even a few words of a foreign language, it is possible to rattle them off with such a beautiful accent that you might be mistaken for a native. The right kind of practice, done in the right frame of mind, can put a near-native accent within anyone's grasp.

Think Sounds, Not Letters

Probably the biggest impediment to good pronunciation is picturing how a word is written while saying it. The written letters are associated in our minds with English sounds. Consequently, these English sounds rise automatically to our lips instead of the foreign ones, and we must spend part of our energy in combatting this tendency. There is nothing hard about saying the French word for "son," which is pronounced "feess"—until you see it written down: *fils*.

Never Look at the Letter *r*

In English, this sound is pronounced differently from other languages. Our tongues curl up more than for a Spanish or Italian *r*, and in quite the opposite direction from a French or German *r*.

Looking at the written word while saying it makes the tongue instinctively take the English *r* position and thereby makes learning the foreign sound more difficult.

The Correct Learning Sequence

The correct learning sequence is this: listen carefully to get the sound firmly planted in your *ear*, then gradually imitate it with your *tongue*. Do not use your *eye* till you have the pronunciation down pat.

The Longer a Word, the Harder

The Spanish word for *nationality* is *nacionalidad*. It has five syllables (na-cio-na-li-dad), none of them particularly difficult to pronounce alone. But the attempt to rattle off this five-syllable word can twist a beginner's tongue. The solution is to break it down into smaller parts and master it piece by piece. However . . .

Start from the End

Instead of saying *na-*, then *-cio-*, and so on, you should begin at the end instead. Say *-dad*, then *-lidad*, etc. You will retain the natural intonation of the word this way, and won't risk swallowing the ending. Try it both ways and see.

Work with a Model

Pronunciation deteriorates easily, so the longer you go without checking yours against a native, the more likely you are to revert to English speech habits. Check your pronunciation often until good speech habits are firmly established in the new language.

Use a Tape Recorder

Every person who studies a foreign language ought to own a light, portable tape recorder. The price of these handy machines, especially of the "cassette" variety, is low enough that virtually anyone can afford one, and it is the handiest gadget imaginable for a language student. Some of the things you can do with a tape recorder that you cannot do without one are:

Have an authentic model to refer to at home.
Learn while traveling, even while driving your car.
Program your own learning and so become your own teacher.
Listen to your own pronunciation and compare it with a native's.
Store tapes for later review.

Some people like to record their language classes so that they can listen to them over and over. Most cassette recorders come equipped with sensitive, unobtrusive microphones that pick up sounds from all parts of a room with astounding clarity.

These machines really come into their own at home, however, where they can be used for studying practically everything: pronunciation, grammar, and vocabulary.

Sample Pronunciation Drills

You may be fortunate enough to record pronunciation drills in the classroom that you can later use at home for additional practice; you also may be able to take adequate drills from the tapes that accompany your textbook. However, just in case you have to (or want to) make your own pronunciation drills, here is a sample to work from. It assumes you can get the cooperation of another person to record the "model" voice; this person should be a native speaker if possible. (Your teacher might well do it for you and others in the class if you make the suggestion.) Failing that, ask another student in the class, one with good pronunciation, to do it for you.

Here is a sequence, which should take about thirty seconds in all, for learning to say the word *nacionalidad* like a native. The same techniques can be used for whole phrases and sentences as well as for single words. First the model speaks, then you repeat in a pause you have left for this purpose, and so on, alternating the model voice and yours:

Model	You
-dad	-dad
-dad	-dad
-dad	-dad
-lidad	-lidad
-lidad	-lidad
-nalidad	-nalidad
-nalidad	-nalidad
nacio-	nacio-
nacio-	nacio-
nacionalidad	nacionalidad

Every Sound Is Important

The wife of a friend of ours, eager to improve her French, located a Frenchwoman and made an appointment to go to her apartment for conversation lessons. She began her first visit by explaining that her French was weak because she had not studied much French grammar. To her surprise, the French lady started to question her about her grandmother. Our friend's wife was mystified, but the conversation continued, and it was not until after the lesson, reflecting on how it had gone, that she realized she must have said *grand'mère* (grandmother) when she meant *grammaire* (grammar). Different as they look on paper, these two French words are only one sound away from being pronounced identically, and she had said the wrong sound.

It is often difficult for people studying a language to understand why their teacher insists on seemingly trivial nuances of pronunciation. If two sounds are so nearly alike that one can hardly hear the difference, why bother learning to distinguish them? It is because, alike as they may seem to a foreigner, each sound is totally different from every other sound to a native speaker of the language; he cannot even imagine how someone can fail to perceive the difference. Did you ever think that "it" could be confused with "eat," or "ship" with "sheep"? Probably not, yet to many foreigners studying English, this distinction seems so faint as to be nearly impossible to master. Many never do master it and so we have the comic book caricature of a foreigner as someone who says, "Geev me theess" for, "Give me this."

Shoot All Problems on Sight

An amusing anecdote will help me make my point. During the 1950s, I traveled to Europe on a Dutch student ship. It was an ex-troopship from World War II, and for $150 you could get a bunk in a dormitory.

During the thirteen-day trip, we passengers got to know some of the Dutch crew fairly well. The one we saw most often was a mess steward whose job was to circulate among the passengers three times a day, at mealtimes, ringing a set of chimes built like a child's xylophone. It had four notes—bong, bong, BONG, bong.

The ship was so full that the passengers had to be fed in two sittings, which doubled the mess steward's work. To announce the noon meal, for example, he would walk around at 12:30, calling out, "First sitting ... first sitting." He would come again at 1:30, calling out, "Second sitting ... second sitting."

The point of the story is that there is no distinction in the Dutch language between the sound *s* and *sh*—if you see what I mean.

For thirteen days, the students on board never tired of teasing him. They pretended to misunderstand so that he would repeat, always with unfailing good humor, calling out the word even louder than before.

If the steward had seriously wanted to learn English, this incident would have happened only once. He would have noticed the merriment his pronunciation was producing, tracked down the reason for it, and practiced until it disappeared. For him, however, there may have been more reward in getting along cheerfully with the passengers than in perfecting his accent, so he did not do so.

Don't Practice Single Sounds

One should not attempt to practice sounds in isolation. To pronounce a French *r* all alone, for example, is not only excessively difficult, it is also unrealistic. When does one ever say a sound all by itself, except for "Oh!" to convey surprise and "Ah!" to indicate admiration?

Always practice sounds in a specific setting. The French *r*, reputedly a very difficult sound, is easier to pronounce in the word *Paris* than in *rouge,* and needs to be practiced in both. The Spanish *r,* too, is harder to pronounce at the beginning of a word (*rojo,* "red") than in the middle (*duro,* "hard"), and in fact is slightly different in each of the following words, depending on the sounds that surround it: *rio, por, para, padre, Francisco, tren.*

Think in Sound-Clusters

Each sound is a little different depending on its setting, because of the way the tongue must glide from one sound to the next. In the French expression *J'en ai un* ("I've got one"), or the Spanish sentence *Voy a hacerlo* ("I'll do it"), you might say each word authentically and yet be unable to glide them together with a native-like accent. One must practice the glide as well as the sounds.

Practice Whole Phrases, Not Words

In real life, a string of words like "I don't know" or "Not on your life" is said as though it were a single word, in one breath-group, without pausing. Similarly, if you stop to take a breath in the middle of a foreign phrase that should be said in a single burst, you are not saying it correctly; you even risk being incomprehensible. Most people think of language as a collection of single words, perhaps because dictionaries are arranged in one-word entries. But what is convenient in a dictionary actually does violence to the reality of language. In practicing pronunciation, it is best to think in terms of word-clusters and to practice the language that way.

Mastering a Difficult Sound

Not long after World War II, I was a student at the Sorbonne and lived in a hotel in the Latin Quarter. I got to know several French students who also lived there, including a young actor and a girl of violent left-wing opinions. The three of us used to get together in the evening, and I was sometimes able to treat them to a rare delicacy like hot chocolate or coffee out of my mother's latest "care" package. Over the drink I would trot out the new words I had learned that day to check whether I understood their meaning and was pronouncing them correctly. I had been in France less than three months, and French was very painful and laborious for me.

One of my hardest sounds was the French *u*. At first I could not say it right at all. Then I grew able to pronounce it in words like *du* and *pure,* but I was still a very long way from saying other words—*rue,* for instance—like a Frenchman. There is an ad in the Paris *Herald Tribune* that instructs the reader how to get to Harry's Bar. It says: "Tell the taxi driver, SANK ROO DOE NOO" (5 rue Daunou). My pronunciation was little better than that, yet I couldn't avoid the word *rue,* for I needed it practically every day to ask directions or exchange addresses with people.

Trying to master the word *rue,* I would walk around repeating it to myself at odd moments, generally aloud—*rue, rue, rue.* In the evening I would ask my two friends if now it was right—and they would say "no" and patiently show me for the millionth time how it ought to sound.

Finally, in desperation, I stumbled onto the "discrimination" method for mastering a really difficult foreign sound. I began to keep careful track of when my friends thought I was closer and when they thought I was further away from the correct pronunciation. (To me it sounded the same all the time, of course.) At last I noticed that when I accidentally produced a kind of high-pitched whistling sound in saying the word, they would say, "There, that's better." From then on it was a matter of training myself to give it this whistling quality all the time. Although I would sometimes backslide out of fatigue, I knew that if I took the trouble I could say it correctly.

The important thing in mastering a difficult sound is to listen very intently, trying to discover what gives it its distinctive quality. Good pronunciation, as I have tried to explain, begins not in the mouth but in the ear.

Invite a Friend to Make Fun of You

When you have trouble hearing the difference between what you are saying and what you ought to say, ask an acquaintance who is a native (or who sounds like one) to imitate your pronunciation followed by the right one. Wrong-right, wrong-right, just like this: *roo/rue . . . roo/rue . . .* over and over. Just listen and try to seize where the difference lies. Don't try saying it yourself prematurely; you risk becoming discouraged easily at this point. Keep listening until you feel the difference penetrating you, and the urge to say it yourself becomes strong. Most likely, you will be in a trance of concentration at that moment, from focusing so hard on a slim difference in sound. Then begin a drill in which you say the word or phrase yourself, with your friend telling you each time whether you are saying it well or badly. Do this for a number of tries, until the "wells" become much more frequent than the "badlys"; but . . .

If You Block, Stop

It is possible to become so drugged with repetitions that the foreign phrase loses all meaning; one becomes transfixed and temporarily unable to go on. If this happens, stop at once and resume your practice at a later time, after a complete change of activity.

Difficult Sounds in Each Language Are Few in Number

I knew a real estate saleswoman in California who felt that her Russian accent was interfering with her business. She told me she was desperately eager to do something about it. I analyzed her speech and found that in point of fact she was making only three or four pronunciation errors. With modest application, she could have eliminated or at least improved them all. But whenever I identified a specific problem for her, she suddenly "lost interest," claiming it was too much trouble to think about correcting it.

Many people react this way. When the discussion of a speech problem becomes too specific, they become psychologically "blocked," and tune out. It might help if they could be convinced that speech problems are not endless, as they often seem, but actually quite few in number, and definitely fixable.

When to Say "the Hell with It"

Pronunciation is important enough that one should try conscientiously to master the authentic foreign accent. One shows respect for foreign people by not making a caricature of their language. Moreover, one is never sure when a pronunciation problem may lead to a misunderstanding, or even to your becoming ludicrous, as the Dutch steward did.

However, there is considerably more to a language than pronunciation. We all know people who immigrated to the United States and have functioned successfully here despite a noticeable foreign accent. Past the age of eighteen, the odds, frankly, are poor that one will ever completely lose the foreign accent. A person's minimal goals should be: (1) to learn all the sounds of the foreign language so as not to risk saying one word for another, and (2) to speak the language with an inoffensive accent. Beyond that, the desire to possess a perfect accent must be weighed against the amount of practice and attention needed to obtain it.

9. How to Master Grammar

An American woman in Mexico does a great deal of work helping Mexicans in rural areas to improve their lot. Her Spanish is fantastically bad. Her verbs are all infinitives and her pronunciation is deplorable. Yet she is eminently successful with government officials, for she goes into a meeting and tries so hard to explain what she wants that the Mexican officials feel sorry for her. Pretty soon they begin to help her plead her cause, and in the process they convince themselves and fellow officials to give her what she wants. For her, it pays to maintain a low level of grammatical performance.

I am not suggesting that one should deliberately learn a language badly, but I do believe that one should concentrate on communicating. If you get your message across, using your hands, eyes, and whatever else you can muster in addition to words, you have a chance to improve your grammar as you proceed. If you insist on correct grammar from the outset, you may well give up out of sheer frustration.

Indeed, foolish insistence on "grammaticalness" as a value in itself is doubtless responsible for more discouragement and failure in language classes than any other factor. It is especially short-sighted when one considers that, in any real-life situation, a person can choose among many alternative ways of getting his meaning across. Someone learning a language needs to learn its grammar, of course—but organically, as part of full interpersonal communication that includes facial expressions, gestures, social conventions, and many other components that may outweigh grammar in importance.

The emphasis should be on communication, and if your teacher does not put it there, then you must do it for yourself. This section will spell out techniques that will help you.

How Much Grammar Is There?

This is a legitimate question for someone undertaking a language to ask, so he can size up the total task before he starts. The rather encouraging answer is that all the grammar a person ever needs to know is covered in a typical year-long college course (two years in high school). After that, further courses merely repeat the same grammar in more complex sentences—sentences that become more literary as you advance, that is, further and further from normal speech.

"Generative" Grammar

Grammar usually is organized along linguistic, not psychological, lines. The grammarian is mainly concerned with the orderliness and internal consistency of his analysis—not its teachableness. Hence, grammar is usually presented in a manner that violates the psychological learning principles mentioned in this book: anticipation, organic learning, the "need to know."

A revolutionary approach to grammar has come into being in recent years that may eventually improve matters. This "generative" approach, often associated with the name of its originator, Noam Chomsky, aims to simulate the process by which native speakers create ("generate") utterances in their language. The past several decades have seen a tremendous surge of interest and activity in this new approach, but largely on the frontiers of pure linguistics. Little that is of practical value has filtered into language textbooks, and Chomsky has stated quite clearly that he doubts whether any applications can be made at the present stage of this new science. As language learners, we are still dependent on traditional grammar.

Fear of Grammar

The word "grammar" strikes terror into many people's hearts, yet in reality the basic grammar of a language is reasonably easy to master. Grammar holds no terror for a three-year-old child as he learns his native language, because he assimilates it unconsciously, intuitively. Like bike-riding or roller-skating, one way to master grammar is by "feel," with very little verbalization of rules. This is a viable alternative (or adjunct) to learning grammar by rules and examples, and since it is less familiar, I want to expound a little on how this intuitive approach works.

Grammar through the Ear

Pierre Delattre, commenting on an experiment he performed where one class learned French grammar by the rules while another learned it by listening to recordings, reported that "students who worked with recordings acquired grammatical habits with unexpected ease. They surmounted problems that looked very intricate in the light of linguistic analysis."

Using a musical analogy, he continued: "Learning grammar from the rules is like learning the interpretation of a melody second-hand from the explanations of someone who has heard it sung. Learning it from direct speech, as with recordings, is like learning the interpretation of a melody directly from hearing it sung. It is the only way to get it fully and exactly.

"After all," Delattre concluded, "the human ear is responsible for what human speech is; and what the ear has done, the ear can understand better than the mind. The ear may find simple what the mind calls complicated."

Grammar through Oral Practice

While teaching French at UCLA, I did an experiment akin to Delattre's that showed vividly the value of an oral approach to grammar.

One of the hardest features of French grammar to teach is the use
of pronouns. They are not difficult in themselves, but the rules about
them are complicated to express.

Je le lui donne means "I give it to him." *Le* is the direct object pronoun; *lui* is the indirect object pronoun.

The traditional way to teach these pronouns is by giving the rules—
first for the direct object, then for the indirect, then for both together.
It often takes a week to ten days to teach pronouns in a college course.

One year, when it came time to teach pronouns, I asked my col-
leagues to let me try an experiment. Certain classes would practice
saying pronoun-filled sentences in the language laboratory, without
hearing any rules, while other ("control") classes would learn them by
the usual method—a statement of rules followed by written and oral
exercises. Then both groups would take the same test.

Though unconvinced, they agreed to let me try the experiment,
knowing they could always teach the rules later on if my oral method
should prove a failure.

The students in the "experimental" group came to the language
laboratory twice. Working with tape recordings, they first repeated
about thirty French sentences containing pronouns. Then they did a
variety of "pattern drills." The tape would say, for example, *Je reçois le
paquet* (I receive the package), and during a pause the student was to
respond with *Je le reçois* (I receive it).

The practice sentences gradually grew more complex until the students could respond to a cue like *Je donne le cadeau à Henri* (I give the
present to Henry) by saying, *Je le lui donne* (I give it to him). During
the two thirty-minute sessions, they heard and said over a hundred
French sentences containing pronouns in various configurations.

Meanwhile, the control classes received conventional instruction.

They learned a rule for direct object pronouns and practiced these for a while, then a rule for indirect object pronouns followed by practice, and finally a rule for both together, with additional practice. Part or all of six class periods was taken up in this way.

The outcome was that, when both groups were tested on their ability to say and write French sentences containing pronouns, the students who had spent only sixty minutes practicing in the lab did slightly better than those who had spent more than a week on it in class.

The reason for their advantage is simple. They had heard and said a large number of correct French sentences, and their ears had become so attuned that only a correct sentence "sounded right" to them. The conventional group, having to rely on the rules, was obliged to figure out each sentence with painstaking care. Not only did this take them longer, but they were much more apt to make trivial errors by slightly misapplying the rules, since they had no "sense of correctness" to fall back on.

This "sense of correctness," lodged in every native speaker's ear through long habituation, enables him instantly to recognize an incorrect sentence when he hears one. As native speakers of English, we have not the slightest doubt that "He is going" is a correct sentence, while "he going" is non-standard but possible (perhaps baby-talk), and "Going he" is impossible. Using this sense, we can instantly identify foreigners and other speakers of non-standard English, and can correct our children when they say "He goed" instead of "He went." A person learning a foreign language needs to develop this same sense, and extensive oral practice is the most direct route to obtaining it.

The other teachers were amazed at the results of the experiment. It convinced them that oral practice can be a viable alternative to conventional grammar, at least for some students, and that oral practice is, at the very least, a precious adjunct to "learning the rules."

Anyone can provide his own oral practice by using a tape or cassette recorder. What one needs to know is how to "program" a language exercise.

By following a simple principle, one can turn a tape recorder into a sophisticated "teaching machine." I call this principle "anticipation" because the learner must anticipate the correct response; he must say it himself before the tape says it. This principle, which I believe to be absolutely basic to learning, merits more discussion.

Anticipation

The best arrangement of material for learning, one that many good teachers use instinctively, is: (1) pose a challenge, (2) let the students try to respond, and (3) provide the correct response.

This principle can be seen in action wherever people are engaged in learning. When Daddy asks his little child how much two and two are, and then starts to give the answer, the child interrupts with, "No, no, Daddy, let me try it myself." He is demanding step two, the pause.

Then the child ventures an answer. "Four," he says, and immediately thereafter, "Is that right, Daddy?" He is demanding step three. And he will not allow Daddy to merely say, "That's right." He insists that the answer be repeated. Daddy must say, "That's right, two and two are four."

The commonest violation of this principle among language teachers is their nagging insistence on repetition. They make students parrot sentences in the foreign language, in the naive expectation that the correct forms will thereby "sink in." But the mind, neurophysiologists tell us, does not function like a wax disk whose grooves wear deeper through repetition. On the contrary, repetition may have a lulling, dulling effect, which, when carried to extremes, becomes hypnotic. A word said over and over many times soon loses all meaning and reverts to a jumble of sounds.

It is novelty that sparks the mind to attention; we perk up our ears at the unexpected. According to one internationally recognized neurophysiologist, H. W. Magoun, the known facts about the workings of the brain "plainly imply that repetition is the first law, not of learning, but of habituation, whose influence upon learning is a negative rather than a positive one. Obviously, the promotion of novelty rather than of repetition should become the primary law of learning."

Novelty means something new, a new challenge. Translated into a formula one can use in studying grammar, the three-step principle of anticipation becomes:

CUE—PAUSE—RESPONSE

To "program" your learning of grammar most efficiently, prepare your own exercises using the three-step formula. First, devise a series of *cues* in the foreign language *that will elicit sentences containing the desired grammar*. Next, record them on your cassette or tape recorder, leaving just enough pause after each cue so that, if you knew the grammar point thoroughly, you could give the answer in the time allowed. Then record the correct response after each pause. This may sound complicated, but an example will show it to be extremely simple.

Let us assume you are a foreign person studying English and that you are working on the past tense of the verb "to go." Your exercise might start like this:

Cue: Are you going to the movies today? (PAUSE)
Response: No, I went yesterday.

Cue: Is your sister going to Europe this year? (PAUSE)
Response: No, she went last year.

Approximately ten such sets of cues and responses make up a "pattern drill," and one or two such drills would impress the past tense of "to go" on you in a matter of a few minutes.

As you progress, your drills will grow more complex, but that does not mean merely using longer sentences. The real secret of learning is gradually to mix together diverse points of grammar—to mix "to go" together with other verbs in the past tense, then with other verbs in other tenses—so that "to go" is elicited *unexpectedly*. The key feature is to have it pop up unexpectedly, thus providing the novelty that accelerates learning.

I can imagine some of my readers' questions. How, you may wonder, can I program exercises in a language I do not know? The answer is that you may find them ready-made in your own textbook, or in another textbook . . . at least in printed form, and perhaps even recorded by natives on tape. Some publishers do provide this sort of aid at present. If not, you must prepare the drills yourself, and there is probably no better way to learn.

You may object that if you go to all the trouble of writing out drills, then there is no real need to record them. However, it is not the same to puzzle over a written sentence till you get it right as it is promptly to answer an interlocutor. One has not really mastered the grammar point until one can use it aloud at something near conversational speed.

If well conceived and carried out at a smart tempo, pattern drills can be a language student's chief tool for learning grammar. This is known to most teachers, but many do not take the trouble to make up the needed drills, or else do not carry them out orally at a rapid pace. So again we come to this: Take charge of your own learning. Program your own study of grammar, and you will have more fun learning the language.

Pronouns

More than 50 percent of the grammar exercises in an elementary language course deal with just two features of grammar: pronouns and verbs. These two frequently cause consternation quite out of proportion to their real difficulty.

Pronouns lend themselves quite naturally to the pattern drill approach. Virtually any question one can ask will bring about the use of a pronoun or two in the answer. Some examples:

Q: Did you see your brother's wife yesterday?
A: Yes, I saw her.

Q: Hasn't Mrs. Dexter lost a lot of weight lately?
A: Yes, she has.

Q: Didn't your father lend his gold watch to the man next door?
A: Yes, he did lend it to him.

The principle is simple enough: make up cues that will force you to use pronouns in the answer. I think most readers will find they can apply this to their specific pronoun-learning problem, with just one proviso: you must forget the old classroom bugaboo about answering in "complete sentences" and give *natural* answers instead.

Verbs

Verbs are the only words in most languages that can assume many forms. In French, for example, a noun can have only two forms (singular and plural), and an adjective only four (masculine singular and plural, feminine singular and plural). But a verb ...! I once counted the different written forms a French verb can take and was amazed to find over 130! Obviously, learning verb forms is one of the most time-consuming tasks in grammar, but fortunately there are ways to make it easier.

REGULAR AND IRREGULAR VERBS. The grammarians' division of verbs into "regular" and "irregular" causes students much unnecessary anguish, for it leads them to believe that language ought to behave perfectly and that "exceptions" are reprehensible outlaws that have somehow escaped the rules.

I prefer to assume instead, like Zorba the Greek, that "life has no exceptions." A living language, like a living person, must be accepted as is, without prejudging how it is going to behave.

Fortunately, the force of an analogy in language is strong; new words tend to form on the model of existing words. It becomes apparent, after a certain number of "irregular" verbs have been learned, that they, too, have regularities in common that make them easier to remember.

A DOZEN KEY VERBAL CONCEPTS. Verbs obey a distinct distribution pattern: a dozen or so common verbs (be, do, go, etc.) account for a very high percentage of all verb occurrences. These few are almost all "irregular," for, being on people's tongues more often, they have evolved and changed form faster.

The dozen key verbal concepts are the following:

to be	to take
to have	to want
to be able	to say or tell
to come	to do or make
to go	to see
to know	to give

Make it one of your earliest jobs to find out how the language you are studying expresses these concepts. (Some of them, like "to be" in Spanish and "to know" in French, may be expressed by more than one verb.) Learn to recognize them in the present and past tenses. After that, through the power of analogy, other "irregular" verbs will fall into place in your mind easily. Meanwhile, knowing these few verbs, you can begin reading the foreign language virtually at once.

LEARN VERBS HORIZONTALLY. Textbooks conventionally separate Romance language verbs into several "conjugations," which they teach separately, one at a time. This is neat and logical in appearance, but psychologically it is all wrong, making verbs harder to learn by stressing their differences rather than their similarities.

Taking three typical French verbs, one from each conjugation, as an illustration, let us look at them in the conventional way, vertically, and in what I regard as the common-sense fashion, horizontally.

Vertical Presentation of French Verbs

1. First conjugation: *laver* ("to wash")

    je lave
    tu laves
    il, elle lave
    nous lavons
    vous lavez
    ils, elles lavent

2. Second conjugation: *finir* ("to finish")

    je finis
    tu finis
    il, elle finit
    nous finissons
    vous finissez
    ils, elles finissent

3. Third conjugation: *vendre* ("to sell")
   je vends
   tu vends
   il, elle vend
   nous vendons
   vous vendez
   ils, elles vendent

Studying these verbs from top to bottom, we get the impression that there are three distinct sorts of verb to be learned. To discover their similarities would require considerable cross-checking.

Here is the same information positioned sideways:

Horizontal Presentation of French Verbs

1	2	3
je lave	je finis	je vends
tu laves	tu finis	tu vends
il, elle lave	il, elle finit	il, elle vend
nous lavons	nous finissons	nous vendons
vous lavez	vous finissez	vous vendez
ils, elles lavent	ils, elles finissent	ils, elles vendent

Reading across, line by line, we discover that each of the six "persons" has a characteristic ending, regardless of which "conjugation" the verb belongs to. The plural endings are identical in all conjugations *(-ons, -ez, -ent)*, and so is the second person singular ending *(-s)*. The *-iss-* inserted in the plural of *-ir* verbs is regular and easy to master. The only learning problems will be the first and third person singular endings, and even here the range of possibilities is very limited: the first person ends either in *-e* or in *-s*, and the third person in *-e*, *-t*, or in nothing.*

---

*In a sense, this explanation is false, because it presents only the *written* forms of French verbs. In speech, several endings are silent and hence the number of forms is

This is not the place to pursue a detailed discussion of French verbs. I merely wish to point out how linguistics has triumphed over psychology in conventional teaching. What the student needs to know is the characteristic written ending that identifies each person of the verb. Clear and simple explanations of grammar points such as this tend to emerge naturally when a teacher adopts an organic, student-centered attitude and lets his grammar explanations be guided by the students' growing "need to know."

What you, as the learner, can do is to construct your own grammar in accordance with your own needs, taking the facts you learn in class or in your book and putting them together to suit your particular learning style.

I urge you to do this even at the risk of making some mistakes. Your eventual goal, after all, is to have in your mind a grammatical schema that will enable you to "generate" utterances in the foreign language. Mistakes are inevitable and unimportant, for this schema is a living, growing organism, and will be fleshed out, modified, and improved as you gain further knowledge of the language.

Learn the Hardest Thing First

I hesitate to bring up the next principle, because it appears to fly directly in the face of reason. Yet it has helped me more than almost any other, so I cannot leave it out.

One assumption about learning is virtually universal. Practically everybody believes that learning must build up gradually from the simple to the complex. Now, what I mean to suggest is that in learning a language one should often do quite the opposite. My principle is this: *Learn the hardest thing first and the rest will then seem easy.*

---

smaller. One of the most heated controversies among language teachers is whether one should present the spoken forms first, the written forms first, or both together. There is much to be said on this subject, and I will not attempt to resolve it here.

The pronoun example provides a good illustration. The "one brick at a time" theory would dictate learning different kinds of pronouns separately before putting them together. Yet in practice it turns out that the sentence with several pronouns ("She gave it to him") is as easy to learn as a sentence with only one pronoun. Perhaps easier.

Similarly, a sentence with two adverbs ("The horse ran exceptionally fast") is hardly more difficult than a sentence with only one ("The horse ran fast"), and furnishes added practice at little added cost. It may in fact be easier to remember because it is more interesting.

The simple-to-complex procedure is psychologically backward; one expends fresh energy on simple things and is fatigued by the time the complex ones arrive. The net result is often a sense of discouragement.

I believe good sense dictates that one should attack the hardest features at the beginning of each lesson, when one is most receptive. The simpler points then tend to fall into place by themselves, and the remainder of the lesson is like coasting downhill.

Gender

In a scene in François Truffaut's poignant film *Jules and Jim,* we see the title characters, a young German and a young Frenchman, sitting before the fire in a Bavarian chalet. The German muses about the gender of words in their two languages:

> Jules: Think of it. Words cannot have the same meaning as they are not of the same sex. In German, war, death, and the moon are masculine, while the sun and love are feminine. Life is neuter.
> Jim: Life? Neuter? That's a nice thought . . . and very logical, too.

Many people hesitate to learn a language partly out of fear of being unable to remember the genders of words, a fear that is largely unjustified.

In the Romance languages, gender is not truly difficult. Most words in Spanish and Italian carry their gender with them, in the final vowel (*-o* for masculine, *-a* for feminine). In French there is no such simple sign, but one quickly acquires a "feel" for gender, and learns helpful rules—for example, that all words ending in *–ion* are feminine (*occupation, notion, discussion,* and so on).

When one forgets the gender of a word, one takes a guess at it. In French, with only two genders, a completely wild guess has a fifty-fifty chance of being right. An "educated" guess of course has a better chance, and you finally get to the point, after some months of studying French, where you have an 80 or 90 percent likelihood of guessing the gender of words correctly.

Not so in German. With three genders (masculine, feminine, neuter), the odds are two-to-one against a wild guess being correct. Though these odds improve with study, the problem remains vexing in German longer than it does in French. This is one of the complexities of German grammar.

Often, however, the problem of gender is more psychological than real. When one is an obvious beginner in the language, foreign people are quite willing to overlook such trifles as a wrong gender; people listen to the meaning of what another person is saying, not to his grammar. Later on, when one knows the language better, one generally finds that one's "feel" for gender has improved along with other progress; the number of errors becomes tolerably small.

The psychological problem here is that mistakes in gender seem to "stick out" in the mind of the person who makes them. A person may massacre verb tenses and use all the wrong order without embarrassment, but if he suddenly realizes he has said "*le maison*" for "*la maison,*" he is mortified.

It should be a consolation to know that even natives do not master gender perfectly. A daily audience-participation show on the French radio is built around a standard type of stickler, which is to telephone a contestant at home and read him a list of eight French words. He is scored on how many words he can give the correct gender. They telephone people in two different towns; the town that knows its genders better is the winner.

Control of gender grows "organically" with increasing mastery of the language. One must guard against the tendency to amplify an occasional lapse out of all proportion to its real importance.

10. How to
Learn Vocabulary

The reader already knows that I consider vocabulary harder to learn than grammar or pronunciation. To become a fairly fluent speaker of a language, with five thousand words at his command, a person would have to learn ten new words a day, day in and day out, for a year and a half. Few people can keep up such a pace; as the vocabulary begins to pile up, one may find oneself forgetting old words almost as fast as one learns new ones. This is a serious problem, but obviously it can be licked. Various devices can help.

Urgency
Sometimes the emotion surrounding a word helps impress it on our memories, especially in a foreign country where all contacts seem to be heightened by newness.

George and Marie arrived in Germany barely a month before their first baby was due. Knowing very little German, Marie was nervous at the prospect of giving birth in a German hospital where the staff, despite their claims to the contrary, spoke virtually no English.

During her stay in the hospital, she found herself learning vocabulary with an ease born of desperation. In a single hearing, she picked up words like *Spritze* (injection), *Narkose* (anesthetic), and *stillen* (breast-feeding). No need to say them over and over; their emotional impact made them stick in her mind after a single hearing.

The same principle may help you. Try to inject a note of urgency into your attitude as you learn vocabulary. Even do it artificially. Later on, the emotional attitude you had at the time of learning may help you to remember.

Often, a life situation can be handled without words, merely by a gesture. Certain movements of the hand or head can mean "Yes," or "I mean *that* one," or "Stop, for heaven's sake!"

Sometimes a single word is required—"later," "good," "hot."

But every so often a traveler runs into a situation where a particular word is crucially needed—one he does not happen to know. That sort of word, once learned, is not easily forgotten.

My cousin Jean, a lively and pretty woman, once took a trip to Italy. Being an art lover, she took the train from Rome to Ravenna to see the mosaics. It was winter. She was the only foreigner on the train.

She was scheduled for a fast change of trains in Bologna, with barely enough time to get from one track to the other. She had a heavy suitcase and needed a porter, but didn't know how to call one in Italian. As she was wrestling with her suitcase, fearful she would miss her connection, an Italian man in her compartment realized her predicament. He pulled open the window, shoved the suitcase out, and held it dangling while he yelled, *"Facchino . . . facchino!"* A porter came running to the window, grabbed the suitcase, and hurried with it to the other train. My cousin had no difficulty remembering the word for porter during the remainder of her trip. She remembers it today, though she has not been back to Italy in more than ten years.

Don't Just Repeat

What one hopes to accomplish in learning vocabulary is to strengthen the bond between stimulus and response—between some life situation that calls for a particular utterance and the utterance itself. To merely repeat without re-creating the situation is almost completely useless. (I say "almost" because some good may be derived from repetition: it may help one's pronunciation.)

If the key to learning is not repetition, what is it? Earlier, I said it was novelty. Now I want to explain how novelty is achieved through randomization.

Randomize

Starting with the ABCs, we are taught as many things as possible in defined orders. The days of the week, the numbers from one to a hundred, the conjugations of verbs. Often we are taught to repeat these by rote, like a litany.

However, some things should be learned *out* of order—or, more precisely, in *random* order. Because that is how we encounter them in life.

Most important is to avoid the "serial order effect"—the cumbersome business of mentally flipping through a whole list till you get to the item you need. If you want to say the number "seven" in a foreign language, it is tedious to have to run through 1, 2, 3, 4, 5, and 6. Or if you want to say "Saturday," you may find you cannot remember it unless you recite the days of the week starting from Sunday. This is the serial order effect.

Knowledge is best when it is free-floating in the mind, available to be recalled at any time, in any order. Learning a list by rote may be a first step—it enables you to drill while walking down the street. But rote practice gives only the illusion of learning, since it does not lead to random command. Practice in random order, though it may appear to take longer, actually economizes time in the long run and provides the most dependable recall. It has been shown that five repetitions randomly spaced have more effect on long-term retention than several times that many done by rote.

Use Flash Cards

One way to translate the principle of random order learning into practice is to use flash cards. These are separate slips of paper or cardboard on which you enter the words you are trying to master. You can make them out of file cards or buy them ready-made ("vis-ed cards") at most school bookstores. Their advantage is that you can reshuffle them at will.

You'll find it fun to invent games while learning. Grouping the cards into "easy" and "hard" piles may give you the enjoyment of seeing one pile diminish and the other grow as you master them. This may keep up your spirits while it cuts your learning time by allowing you to go through the "hard" pile more often than the "easy" pile. Total study time is reduced; you are putting in effort only where it is needed.

It is better to write a whole phrase on the flash cards than a single word, for a phrase is not much harder to learn and is very much more useful. Some psychologists even contend that a phrase is not harder at all, because, they say, the mind "encodes" it as if it were a single word. They point out that people learn number sequences as if they were a single unit (the numbers 1, 4, 9, 2 become "fourteen ninety-two") and word sequences as if they were single words (the four words keep/off/the/grass become "Keep-off-the-grass").

Phrases are more serviceable than single words because they are ready to go to work without further adaptation. If you are studying English, and you learn the phrase "Give me a menu, please," you can use it as is when you go to a restaurant. You also may be able to combine parts of it with pieces of other phrases already learned. By substituting for the word "menu," for instance, you can produce sentences like: "Give me a screwdriver, please," or "Give me a timetable, please." Or you can insert other phrases into the same slot, producing new utterances like: "Give me a bowl of soup, please," or "Give me that pair of shoes, please."

Write on your flash cards a phrase or sentence that shows a typical usage. If you are studying French and want to learn the word for wine, make up a flash card with a phrase like *du vin blanc* (some white wine) or *Je préfère le vin rouge* (I prefer red wine).

Similarly, if you wish to learn a grammatical expression—let's say *jusqu'à* (until)—put it down on a flash card in a sentence like *Il est resté jusqu'au matin* (He stayed until morning). The more striking or entertaining your sentence is, the better you are apt to recall it.

Vary the English Side

A typical list of foreign language vocabulary to be learned looks like this:

> night—*la nuit*
> day—*le jour*
> happy—*heureux*
> question—*la question*
> answer—*la réponse*

... and so on. However, this is *not* the way your flash cards should look, for at least two good reasons. You do not want to pair up French words with English words lest you be able to recall *la nuit* only when thinking "night." Rather, you want *la nuit* to occur to you when you are "thinking in French," without having to go through English to remember it. Secondly, you want to practice the word *nuit* in the very situations in which you might have to use it.

Hence, you make several flash cards (or several lines on one), using each word in several different typical contexts. For *la nuit*, you might make three cards, reading:

English Side	*French Side*
I never go out at night.	*Je ne sors jamais la nuit.*
Good night.	*Bonne nuit.*
I slept badly last night.	*J'ai mal dormi cette nuit.*

Mix those cards in with the others so they'll come up in random order. Once you can deliver the French sentence in response to these three different stimuli, you "know" *la nuit* in a much richer sense than if you could say it only in response to the English word "night."

Program Your Memory

I once heard a teacher say to a class: "You mustn't forget the sentence patterns we learned last week. You must apply them constantly." Where, I wondered, were they supposed to apply them, when their only contact with the language was in the class? It was the teacher's job to keep them from forgetting, not just warn them to remember.

I maintain that a student's memory is largely the teacher's responsibility. This is a novel notion, for most people believe that memory is a private matter and that if a person forgets what he has learned it is no one's fault but his own. I will explain what I mean.

One value of flash cards is that they can be randomized easily, by shuffling them. The words will then come up unexpectedly, by chance. Suppose, however, that instead of depending on chance, you could "program" the cards so that each word came up at just the right moment to ensure the longest retention with the fewest exposures? Such a program would be worth a lot, for it would reduce your study time to a minimum while virtually guaranteeing maximum retention.

There is a program, which I call "graduated interval recall." Here is how it works.

Let us suppose that you have just this instant learned a new vocabulary word. Follow closely what happens as you commit it to memory. First, you repeat it a few times, adjusting the pronunciation. You may tell yourself you want to remember it, but then you go on to think about other things, and as you do, *the word you have just learned starts fading rapidly*. If you try to think of it again after five minutes have passed, you will probably find it is no longer in your mind. This is depressing. ("Damn, I forgot it; I don't have any memory for these foreign words.")

But suppose you had not let the memory fade for five minutes? Suppose you had tested yourself again after a few seconds? The chances of your remembering would have been very much greater.

Now the secret: If you program your study correctly, then every time you revive an item, you make it harder to forget.

If you test yourself after five seconds, thereby reviving your memory of the new word, then you can let it go a little longer before reviving it again (perhaps half a minute), still longer the next time (perhaps one and a half minutes), and so on until you remember it indefinitely.

This principle can be visualized on a timeline. In Figure 1 on the next page, the solid lines represent intervals of time during which you are not thinking about the item but are paying attention to other tasks.

The principle of graduated interval recall says that if you refresh your memory frequently at first, you will need to do so less and less often as time passes.

Follow the Natural Frequencies

One of the quickest and surest ways to pick up foreign vocabulary is through reading. There is a richness of association in reading, which aids the memory, and "organic" learning is facilitated by the natural progression of word frequencies.

Figure 1. Graduated Interval Recall Schedule

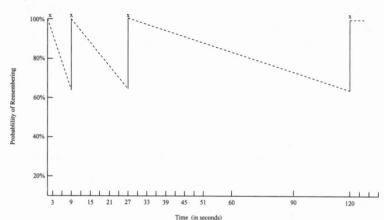

As you read, the words you notice first are automatically the most frequent, most useful words: they appear most often. These are the words to learn first, skipping over other, less frequent words for the moment.

When you feel that you have seen a certain word before and are tired of skipping over it without knowing its meaning, then it is time to look it up. The word may almost seem to thrust itself up off the page at you; this is your signal to stop and learn it, because at that moment you have strong, positive motivation that will help you to remember.

You may also have negative motivation. Thumbing a dictionary is mildly punitive, especially when you are caught up in reading an interesting page. You are obliged to interrupt your enjoyment, lay the book down, pick up a dictionary, and perform a tedious alphabetic search. The desire to avoid this tiresome process can motivate you to confine your searching to words you really need to know. Once having looked them up, it can make you determined not to forget them so as not to have to do it again.

Above all, reading is a pleasure. The delight of reading—in the original—a play by Molière, a novel by Dostoyevsky, an essay by Freud, or an article on your favorite subject is one of the chief rewards for learning a language. It is also one of the most accessible. Reading, by far the simplest skill to master, is chiefly a matter of learning enough vocabulary to "pass the hump."

"Passing the Hump"

Let us take a hypothetical foreign person learning to read English. If he uses the approach I am recommending here, and learns the most frequent words first, he will find that after learning only one hundred words, every second word on the average printed page will look familiar to him. He will not, of course, be able to comprehend, but it is nevertheless important to realize that the one hundred commonest English words actually account for 50 percent of the vocabulary in a typical English book.

Look back at the first sentence of the preceding paragraph, beginning "Let us take . . ." It contains eleven words. Five of them (us, take, a, to, read) are among the two hundred most frequent English words. Three more (let, person, English) are nearly as frequent; they figure among the five hundred commonest words. Two of the remaining words (learning, foreign) are only slightly less common; they are among the two thousand commonest words. Only one word in that sentence is rare: "hypothetical." In one frequency study of five million words of English prose, "hypothetical" occurred only once.

As our foreigner's basic vocabulary increases, his reading comprehension mounts sharply. When he knows five hundred words, he will be able to recognize two-thirds of the words in most written texts;

when he knows a thousand words, he will recognize three-fourths, and so on, until by the time he knows five thousand words, fully 98 percent of printed matter will look familiar to him. Figure 2 below illustrates the relationship of word frequency to word occurrence.

Figure 2. Relationship of Word Frequency to Word Occurrence

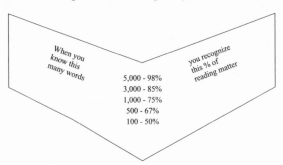

When you know this many words

you recognize this % of reading matter

5,000 - 98%
3,000 - 85%
1,000 - 75%
500 - 67%
100 - 50%

However, our hypothetical foreigner will clearly not be reading fluently as long as he still must look up every fourth or fifth word he meets. Reading will not cease being drudgery until he can read at least a few sentences without reaching for a dictionary. What we want to know is when this crossover point, this "hump," may be reached.

"Guessability"

English will become easy for our foreigner to read when he can guess, infer, or somehow figure out the meaning of most new words he meets from the words he already knows: When he can understand "occupation," though he has never seen it, because he knows the word "occupy." When he can understand "leadership" because he knows "leader," and "Grandma" because he knows "grandmother."

This is the "hump" in learning foreign vocabulary. After passing it, reading grows to be its own reward, and it becomes a simple and pleasurable event to add an occasional new word to an already substantial vocabulary.

The "hump," where new words grow "guessable," is reached more quickly in some languages than in others.

Passing the "Hump" in German

When I was in high school, my friends and I went through a period of "vocabulary building." We would spend part of each evening poring over books like *Build Your Word Power,* storing up esoteric words to "stick" each other with on the way to school the next day. Like most Americans, I grew up believing it was important to have a large vocabulary.

That is why I was astounded when I learned, years later, that all educated people in Germany have essentially the same vocabulary. The German language builds its words out of a relatively small stock of basic components. Every German knows them all by the time he finishes high school; hence every German high school graduate has essentially identical vocabulary. The only way to "stick" an educated German on a vocabulary test is to ask him archaic or foreign words.

The vocabulary "hump" is reached earlier in German than in most other languages. The thousand most frequent German words actually comprise about 80 percent of most reading matter; the second thousand words raise this figure to 90 percent.

Still, even 90 percent recognizability would not be sufficient for fluent reading if one had to look up each unfamiliar word—one in ten. What makes German relatively easy is that after one has made the initial effort of learning the most frequent words, new words become so highly "guessable" that they are usually obvious without consulting a dictionary. The "hump" in German is passed when one knows fifteen hundred to two thousand words; and many of those, we must remember, look at least vaguely familiar because of their similarity to English words.

Passing the "Hump" in French

The French guessing game in an earlier section demonstrated that an American can guess about 30 percent of French words without having studied the language. As he studies French, his guessing rate goes up in a steady progression (as shown in Table 3 below), until it reaches 80 percent and levels off at that rate.

Table 3. "Guessability" of French Words

Number of Words You Know	Percentage of Words You Can Guess
500	35%
1,000	50%
2,000	60%
3,000	70%
4,000	75%
5,000	80%

A person can read French with ease as soon as he has a vocabulary of about three thousand words and can guess the meaning of unfamiliar words with 70 percent accuracy. One is not free of the dictionary, however, until he knows nearly five thousand words, at which point he still meets a small number of unfamiliar words but can either figure them out from the context or, as with the names of specific flowers and berries, for example, may be willing to let them go. However, that five thousand figure includes a heavy proportion of words that are identical to English words or similar enough that they are recognizable and easily learned. As in German, the "hard-core" problem in learning to read French probably comes down to learning about fifteen hundred to two thousand non-cognate words.

These patterns of German and French vocabulary point to certain general conclusions about learning vocabulary in the Teutonic and Romance languages: (1) Learn the commonest words first because they will accelerate your guessing power; (2) begin reading as soon as you have learned five hundred to a thousand common words; (3) pick reading material that interests you strongly and continue to learn words following the natural frequencies.

If you are willing to make the initial thrust to learn a few hundred common words, you can be reading the foreign language, though slowly, within two to three months, and reading with reasonable fluency within six. This can be your first major accomplishment in learning the language, one that pays dividends in reading pleasure, and helps boost your vocabulary for learning to speak and write. This is no pipe dream. Solid facts say that by using this strategy, whether in a class or on your own, you can be well along in a foreign language six months from today.

Conclusion

11. Beyond the Spoken Word

The Silent Language

- Never talk to a Chinese businessman with your hands on your hips. He will think you are angry at him.
- When sitting with Moslems, do not extend the soles of your feet (or shoes) in the direction of others. It is very impolite.
- Latin Americans like to talk up close, about a foot from nose to nose, while any distance less than two feet makes a North American think he is about to be kissed. When talking to a Latin American, you may find yourself back-pedaling across the room, with him in pursuit.

There is so much more to language than mere words. Each language has its own repertory of gestures, facial expressions, and body movements—wordless signs that E. T. Hall has called "the silent language." When you are conversing with native speakers, such non-verbal means of communication are often vitally important. Ignoring them is apt to cause you trouble in getting across your message, as the examples just given illustrate.

Role-playing

An acquaintance of mine named Jerry was studying Tagalog in preparation for a trip to the Philippines. I talked to him about the "silent language," and advised him to play the role of a Filipino to the hilt during his lesson by using Filipino gestures and expressions as well as words.

Jerry's study group included four other students and two Filipino women who served as "native informants." The group used a method developed at the Foreign Service Institute. They learned conversational dialogues by heart, the technique being to go around the table repeating one sentence at a time, then two sentences, and so on until everyone had more or less mastered it. The native informants were there to correct anyone whose pronunciation dropped below an acceptable standard.

On that particular day, the group was doing a new dialogue that everyone found difficult. Certain sentences were long and complicated, and none of the students was able to capture the native intonation. As the dialogue went round the table, Jerry remembered my advice and decided to try role-playing.

He closed his eyes and concentrated on "psyching" himself into the skin of a Filipino. He imagined how he might look: short and wiry, not much over five feet two, with a yellow or brown complexion. He saw himself standing on a street corner in Manila; it was very hot; he was dressed in a loose white shirt and chino pants; the shirt was starched and worn outside the trousers. Jerry had worked summers in a resort hotel with Filipino waiters and he conjured them up in his mind to add realism to this portrayal.

All the while, the conversation was going around the table, with each person saying two sentences and receiving corrections. When Jerry's turn came, he threw himself into the role. Tossing caution to the winds, he blurted out the two sentences as he imagined a Filipino person would.

The informants stopped the lesson, and for the first time said, "There. That was very, very good. That was authentic."

Jerry had done something brave. He had cast off his own natural behavior—his identity—and taken on that of a Filipino. In doing so, he had risked sounding and looking ridiculous.

That is the kind of risk you should be prepared to take if your objective is to learn a language really well. Letting yourself play the role of a foreigner will improve your performance. It may help you to hurdle pronunciation problems that had been getting you down before. It also will enliven the class for you. During moments of boredom, you may gradually imagine your new, foreign self in more detail: your job, your family, your boyfriend or girlfriend.

Psychologist Carl Rogers, in his inspiring book *Freedom to Learn*, says, "I find that one of the best, but most difficult, ways for me to learn is to drop my own defensiveness, at least temporarily, and to try to understand the way in which his experience seems and feels to the other person." The willingness to risk dropping one's own identity may be the crucial factor that enables certain people to learn a foreign language like a native.

Handling Embarrassing Moments

The "silent language" can produce some awkward moments when one first arrives in a foreign country.

My wife and I were looking for an apartment in Athens. We had been there only a few days and knew pitifully little Greek. From the first day, we noticed a peculiar reaction. When I went up to a newsstand, for example, and asked the man for the *Herald Tribune*, he nodded his head up and down, apparently indicating that he had it, but made no move to hand it over. After waiting for a few minutes and receiving no newspaper, I finally walked away, perplexed.

At the first apartment building we went to, we rang the bell, the superintendent came to the door, and we bashfully said the sentence we had learned by heart: "Have you an apartment for rent?" The man looked at us amiably—all Greeks are friendly and helpful to foreigners—and nodded his head up and down. He seemed to be saying that he had an apartment for rent, and we expected to be invited in to inspect it. We stood looking at him, he stood looking at us, all of us getting more and more embarrassed, until finally we walked away, utterly bewildered.

After three such incidents happened in a single day, we at last realized the problem. When a Greek nods his head up and down, he does not mean yes, he means no.

Saying no is a rich ceremony in Greek, with a set of hand and eye movements that are inimitable and highly expressive. When a Greek person says no, he rolls his eyeballs skyward, raises his eyebrows, clicks his tongue, and lifts both hands, palms up. He seems to be calling on the Olympian gods to witness how sorry he is to have to say no instead of yes.

Our embarrassment in Athens was mild, however, compared with what a person feels who realizes after the fact that he has uttered a gigantic howler and can never take it back. This happened to an Israeli student shortly after his arrival in Austin, Texas, where he planned to attend the university. He had just come to America and his English was weak. One day he noticed that a button had fallen off his jacket. To sew it back on, he needed to ask his landlady for a needle and thread.

Rehearsing the conversation in his mind, he was almost certain he knew the word "needle." He did not know the word "thread," but was confident he could get the idea across.

He went downstairs and knocked on the landlady's door. "Come in," said the elderly Texas lady. "Can I help you?"

"Yes," replied the student, "I'd like a noodle and rope."

Keep Quiet

There are times in a foreign country when you should sit there and keep your mouth shut.

Rhoda was spending a year in Germany after graduating from college. She wanted to find a job that would bring her in contact with Germans, and applied to teach English in a private language school. Her German was not very good, but the job interview would be in English, or so she assumed.

When she arrived, she was ushered into the office of the directress, an imposing Russian lady who spoke German with a heavy accent . . . and no English at all. While shaking hands, Rhoda muttered a few carefully prepared words of greeting. She sat down opposite the directress, who, to Rhoda's immense relief, launched into a lengthy explanation of how she had founded the school and the kinds of students it attracted. Rhoda sat and listened as though she understood, nodding amiably from time to time to renew the flow of words. After twenty minutes, a secretary interrupted to say that the directress was wanted on the phone. She quickly complimented Rhoda on her knowledge of German, told her she was hired, and showed her out of the office.

Keep Talking

There also may be times when all you can do is keep talking.

An older woman I know tells of the time when, as a young girl, she was invited to visit a foreign warship docked in San Diego harbor. Her escort was a handsome naval officer. After they had toured the ship, he invited her for a drink in the officers' lounge. They sat there for more than an hour, during which time he never ceased talking. He went on and on about anything that came into his mind, and though he was charming, his compulsive talking finally began to bore her. She interrupted to compliment him, somewhat ironically, on his fluent command of English. He must have sensed her annoyance, for he explained that he had learned English in his native country, Portugal, and had never spent any time in any English-speaking country. He talked a lot, he said, because he could speak the language but could not understand it. He feared that if he stopped for even a moment, she would surely say something that he would not understand.

Take It on the Chin

Practically everyone who has gone abroad has had embarrassing moments like those I recounted. My own "most embarrassing moment" remains with me to this day, though it happened years ago.

I was twenty, and going to Europe for the first time. Though I had taken French for three years in high school, I could not speak a word of it.

All during the eight-day boat trip, I practiced saying the first sentence I imagined I would need when I arrived in Paris—the address of the hotel where I was going to stay. I repeated it to myself over and over: *Deux cent vingt-cinq rue Saint-Jacques* ("225 rue Saint-Jacques").

When the boat landed, things went nearly as I had imagined. We docked at Le Havre and took the boat-train to Paris, arriving at the Saint-Lazare railroad station. I found a line of people waiting for taxis, and joined them with my baggage. Waiting my turn, I practiced my precious sentence.

At last my turn came. I climbed into the backseat of the taxi, the driver turned and looked at me over his shoulder, and I delivered my well-rehearsed line: *Deux cent vingt-cinq rue Saint-Jacques.*

He showed no sign of comprehending. Instead, he asked me in English, with a broad French accent, "Whaire do you weesh to go, monsieur?"

Sheepishly, I told him the address in English and sat back, too miserable to enjoy my first glimpses of Paris.

Keeping the Waitress Waiting

Sometimes people create their own problems.

Charles and Amy walked into a sweetshop in Salzburg, Austria, to have some ice cream. The shop was located near the Festival Hall, and Charles noticed a display of programs on the wall autographed by singers and conductors from the Salzburg Music Festival. While he detoured to examine them, the waitress behind the counter looked up expectantly, prepared to take their order.

Amy prodded her husband and said in a low voice, "She's waiting."

Charles was annoyed that his wife seemed more concerned about the waitress than about his interests. He lashed out, too loudly for politeness, "The hell with her, let her wait," and continued inspecting the music programs.

Amy stomped out of the shop, furious with him for embarrassing her in public. Soon Charles followed, furious with her for insisting that he do the "right" thing rather than the thing that interested him. After about half an hour they patched up the quarrel and continued their visit to Salzburg.

Soon it was dinner time and they went to a typical Austrian restaurant, their argument not entirely forgotten. The waitress brought the menu, then took out her pad and pencil, obviously waiting for them to order. Amy immediately began feeling awkward. Without taking time to study the menu, she ordered the first thing that caught her eye. Then she regretted it, so Charles called the waitress back and told her they were not sure what they wanted. Again the waitress stood there, waiting for them to make up their minds. And again the pressure was such that they could not study the menu but placed a quick order, just to relieve the tension.

The waitress was a simple person from an Austrian village. There was nothing imposing about her, nor had she really *done* anything other than give prompt service. Yet her presence had made them acutely uncomfortable and nearly rekindled an argument that would have spoiled their dinner.

How had she gotten the power to do all this? Evidently, *they gave it to her.* By believing that they had to order quickly and dare not keep her waiting, they had allowed her to tyrannize them though that was not her intention in the least.

Everyone who goes abroad inevitably finds himself in such situations and should be armed in advance to cope with them. One should learn how to say, "I'm not ready to order yet," or "Come back in five minutes," or whatever ploy one favors. One should arm oneself, too, with an attitude—that one will remain in command of the situation and not succumb to embarrassment despite the psychological disadvantage of being a stuttering foreigner.

One easily feels like an underdog in a foreign country. It is their country and their language, and one worries at every turn about inadvertently committing some rudeness. This feeling is inescapable, and it is a good idea to consciously build defenses against it before going abroad.

Picking Up Clues

A Greek travel agent in New York once said to me in the course of a conversation, "There will be too many people in Greece this summer."

I thought that was an odd remark for a travel agent to make, especially as he said it with a pleased smile, obviously happy that his business was prospering.

What he meant was, "There will be many people in Greece this summer." The Greek language makes no distinction between "many" and "too many"; the word *polli* has both meanings.

I wanted to give him an opportunity to improve his English, so I deliberately responded with puzzlement. I asked, "How can there be too many, since the tourist business helps the Greek economy?"

He had been in business in New York for four years. Probably others had reacted in a puzzled way before. But he had not picked up their clues and did not pick up mine. Perhaps his "organic" learning of English was not yet ready to perceive this error. Or else his English had leveled out on a plateau where further progress was improbable.

Certain clues simply cannot be ignored, however. My neighbor once took a trip to Spain. He planned to go boar hunting, which required an official permit from a ministry in Madrid. In the course of obtaining it, he was sent from one office to another and another. In each he said the same sentence, painstakingly constructed from a pocket dictionary, and each time was met by a gale of laughter. After the third or fourth time, he finally asked an English-speaking person what was wrong. He found out that while he intended to say, "I want to hunt a pig" (*Quiero cazar un cerdo*), he had been saying, "I want to marry [*casar*] a pig" instead.

The moral is: When a strange reaction follows something you have said, always track down the reason. Never let a chance go by to correct a wrong habit; these mistakes are finite in number and it is possible to correct them all.

Getting to Know You

One reason, perhaps the biggest, why people travel to foreign countries is that they want to understand themselves better though understanding others. We may find out who we are and how we got to be that way by observing people who have been molded differently by another environment. The contract is sharpest where the country's social and political system departs most from our own. For many Americans, this is the fascination of a trip to Russia.

Fred Jenkins, a junior executive in an oil company, was visiting Russia on a twenty-day tour. He had studied Russian for a year in college, and, though he could not hold a fluent conversation, he could manage to ask for borscht, buses, and the bathroom. This gave him confidence enough to go off from the group. He wanted to "get a feel" for the country and the people.

He was first surprised, then offended by the rudeness he sometimes encountered. When he went to the post office to mail a package, he held out his package and asked if he could mail it. The answer was an abrupt *Nyet!* (No!). No explanation; no advice on how to go about it. Just *Nyet!* With a scowl.

Later that day he wanted a glass of tea. It was nearly closing time at the tearoom, and a large, buxom woman stood blocking the door. Fred asked her in broken Russian if he could go in for a glass of tea, promising to drink it quickly and leave. Her answer, in an unequivocal tone of voice, was *Nyet*.

Up to then Fred had accepted these rebuffs in the polite, submissive manner a traveler tends to adopt in a foreign country to avoid giving offense. But he was growing angry at being shouted at and pushed around. He decided to see what would happen if he returned this treatment in kind.

He went back to the tearoom, where the woman was still guarding the door. Again he asked if he could have a glass of tea, and again was glared at and told *Nyet*. This time, instead of going away, he began arguing in halting but aggressive Russian, reinforced by vigorous gestures. He shouted that this was a fine way to treat a visitor, that all he wanted was a glass of tea and would not hold up their closing time, and so on. After a moment's hesitation, the woman stepped aside and let Fred squeeze by her into the tearoom. She turned and called over her shoulder to the waitress (in Russian), "Give him a glass of tea." During the remainder of his stay in Russia, Fred made it a point to argue with every *Nyet*, and was amazed how often he got what he wanted.

I do not, of course, recommend deliberate rudeness, but I do suggest that a person who goes abroad should be prepared to try out different modes of behavior in interacting with native people. Their reactions will not always be those we expect, and a certain amount of fumbling is inevitable as we search for communication. Quite often, as in the following incident, the result may be a warm experience, perhaps even a cherished memory.

The Istanbul Hilton is the favorite stopping place for many Americans visiting Turkey. But my wife, Beverly, and I wanted to get to know the city of Istanbul, and thought we might do better elsewhere. When we arrived at the railroad station, instead of heading for the Hilton in a taxi, we checked our baggage and set off on foot in the teeming port area near the station to look for a suitable hotel.

We took the wider, more easily passable streets, and saw many unusual sights. On one back street, a row of men were sitting on a curb outside a building. Each one had a saddle strapped to his back. They were porters waiting for business, the human equivalent of pickup trucks. Using the saddles, they could carry towering piles of packages and merchandise, mountainous loads that seemed ready to cascade down at any moment.

We were still musing over the implications of using men as beasts of burden, when we came upon a hotel that looked quite new. We went in to ask about a room. They gave us the pick of the house; the hotel had just opened and the first guests, a busload of Yugoslavian tourists, were not scheduled to arrive for a week. We said we would like a view of the Bosphorus, and were assigned a room on the top floor, the fifth.

The entire personnel of the hotel appeared to consist of the manager, who could understand a little French, and a porter, who spoke only Turkish.

With many smiles and courteous gestures, the porter took us up in the elevator, showed us to our room, and left. The room turned out to be clean and modern, and it had windows on every side. More windows, in fact, than we had counted on, for although they did provide a lovely view of the Bosphorus, they opened out directly onto corridors and rooftops that to us, strangers in Istanbul, looked anything but safe. We felt, especially after dark, that we were living on a small airy island surrounded by dangers.

While preparing for bed, we discovered that the hot water had not yet been turned on in the hotel, pending the arrival of the Yugoslavs. We quickly adjusted to washing in cold water, but the next morning, shaving proved to be a problem. I picked up the telephone—during the first, uneasy night, the telephone had come to seem like our only link with the outside world—and when the porter answered, I asked for some hot water. No reply. I tried French: *eau chaude*. Still no answer. Then I commenced thumbing the section of "useful words and phrases" in my guidebook with one hand, while juggling the receiver with the other, and making occasional grunting sounds to keep the porter from hanging up.

According to the guidebook, the word for "hot" was *sicak* and the word for "water" was *su*. I remembered having read somewhere that the letter *c* is pronounced like *j* in Turkish, so I said to the porter, *Su sijak!* Then the lightbulb lit up, and in a triumph of sudden comprehension, he said, *Sijak su! Sijak su!* I rushed to give him confirmation: *Yes, yes, yes, oui, oui, oui*. He then said something in Turkish, which I hopefully took to mean that he was going to bring me hot water, and hung up.

About five minutes later, the elevator door clanked and we heard footsteps approaching our fishbowl room. I was at the door before he knocked. The porter, still beaming with the joy of understanding my request, was carrying a small metal teapot with a wisp of steam rising from its spout. It was only a fraction of the quantity of water I would have liked, but it seemed infinitely precious to me. I beamed back at him, gave him a tip, and closed the door.

As I stood there with the tiny teapot of water, I realized that something special had taken place between the porter and me. Through our struggle to communicate, we had felt a rush of good fellowship for each other.

This feeling lasted for the remainder of our five-day stay. Each morning I would pick up the telephone and say, with growing confidence, *Sijak su*. And the response would come, warm and reassuring, *Sijak su*. Five minutes later, the tiny teapot would be brought to my door. When we left the hotel, the porter and I shook hands with sincere affection. We had shared an experience.

Answer Key for Quiz on "Guessable" French Words (page 11)

1	2	3	4	5
brother	course	happiness	existence	day after
garden	plan	guard	detail	will
sentiment	role	value	anger	walk
scene	bad luck	habit	drawing room	madam
situation	envy	blood	newspaper	crowd
tree	place	color	flower	boy
impression	king	subject	mouth	gesture
tear	frank	title	rapport, relationship	society
taste	field	care	faith	room
law	importance	fault, lack	group	joy

Appendix 1
Languages of the World

In this list, the world is divided into five regions: Africa, America, Europe, Near East, and Far East. Within each region, countries are listed alphabetically with their capitals. In many countries, the languages spoken in major cities other than the capital differ from those used in the capital. When this is the case, the additional information for these cities is also provided.

Principal languages are listed in the second column. These are indigenous languages, either official or nonofficial, used by a significant segment of the population.

Other languages are listed in the third column. These are either non-indigenous world languages used widely by the government and in educated circles or any languages other than a principal language that is useful in communicating with a substantial segment of the population or with a significant minority group.

Style within Entries

Parentheses indicate regional variants, which may or may not be mutually intelligible. Examples: Chinese (Mandarin), Chinese (Cantonese).

A *slash* indicates that two different names are used for the same language.

A *hyphen* distinguishes mutually intelligible variants. Examples: Serbo-Croatian; Zulu-Xhosa.

Arabic, which has many regional variations, some mutually intelligible and some not, is divided into Eastern and Western.

Chinese is divided into six regional variations: Amoy-Swatow, Cantonese, Fuchow, Hakka, Mandarin, and Wu. While these languages are not mutually intelligible in spoken form, speakers can communicate in writing owing to their common pictographic writing system.*

*Help in updating was provided by William W. Gage of the Center for Applied Linguistics, Washington, D.C.

Country & City	Principal Languages	Other Languages
The Americas		
Antigua St. John's	English	
Argentina Buenos Aires	Spanish	Italian
Bahamas Nassau	English	
Barbados Bridgetown	English	
Belize Belmopan	English Spanish	Mayan (Yucatec)
Bermuda Hamilton	English	
Bolivia La Paz	Spanish	Aymara Quechua
Brazil Brasília	Portuguese	
British Virgin Islands Road Town	English	

Country & City	Principal Languages	Other Languages
Canada		
Ottawa	English	French
Montréal	French	
	English	
Québec	French	English
Cayman Islands		
Georgetown	English	
Chile		
Santiago	Spanish	
Concepción	Spanish	Araucanian
		German
Colombia		
Bogotá	Spanish	
Costa Rica		
San José	Spanish	
Cuba		
Havana	Spanish	
Dominica		
Roseau	English	
	French Patois	
Dominican Republic		
Santo Domingo	Spanish	
Ecuador		
Quito	Spanish	Quechua

Country & City	Principal Languages	Other Languages
El Salvador San Salvador	Spanish	
Falkland Islands Stanley	English	
French Guiana Cayenne	French French Creole	
Grenada St. George's	English French Patois	
Guadeloupe Basse-Terre	French French Creole	
Guatemala Guatemala	Spanish	Quiche Kakchikel Mam Kekchi
Guyana Georgetown	English	Spanish Hindi Urdu
Haiti Port-au-Prince	French Haitian Creole	

Country & City	Principal Languages	Other Languages
Honduras Tegucigalpa	Spanish	
Jamaica Kingston	English	
Martinique Fort-de-France	French French Creole	
Mexico Mexico City	Spanish	
Montserrat Plymouth	English	
Netherlands Antilles Willemstad	Dutch Papiamento	Spanish English
Nicaragua Managua	Spanish	
Panamá Panamá	Spanish	English
Paraguay Asunción	Spanish Guaraní	
Peru Lima	Spanish	Quechua

Country & City	Principal Languages	Other Languages
Puerto Rico San Juan	Spanish English	
St. Christopher- Nevis-Anguilla Basseterre	English	
St. Lucia Castries	English French Patois	
St. Pierre & Miquelon St. Pierre	French	
St. Vincent Kingstown	English	
Suriname Paramaribo	Sranan Hindi Javanese Dutch	English Spanish
Trinidad & Tobago Port-of-Spain	English	Hindi
Turks & Caicos Islands Grand Turk	English	

Country & City	Principal Languages	Other Languages
United States Washington, D.C.	English	Spanish
Uruguay Montevideo	Spanish	Italian Portuguese
Venezuela Caracas	Spanish	

Europe

Albania Tirana	Albanian	
Andorra Andorra la Vella	Catalan	
Austria Vienna	German	Serbo-Croatian Slovak Hungarian Czech
Azores Ponta Delgada	Portuguese	
Belgium Brussels	Dutch-Flemish French	German Italian

Country & City	Principal Languages	Other Languages
Bulgaria		
Sofia	Bulgarian	Turkish
		Romany
Czechoslovakia		
Prague	Czech	Slovak
		German
		Russian
Bratislava	Slovak	Czech
		German
		Hungarian
		Romany
Denmark		
Copenhagen	Danish	German
		English
England		
London	England	
Finland		
Helsinki	Finnish	Swedish
		English
France		
Paris	French	*

*Immigrant workers are a significant part of the population. The languages represented may vary over the years. Currently, in Paris, Spanish, Portuguese, Italian, and Arabic (Western) are important. In Germany, Italian, Spanish, Greek, Turkish, and Serbo-Croatian are found. In Luxembourg, Portuguese is predominant.

Country & City	Principal Languages	Other Languages
Germany, East (German Democratic Republic)		
East Berlin	German	Polish
Germany, West (German Federal Republic)		
Bonn	German	*
Gibraltar		
Gibraltar	English Spanish	
Greece		
Athens	Greek	French
Greenland		
Godthaab	Danish Greenlandic	
Hungary		
Budapest	Hungarian	German Slovak
Iceland		
Reykjavik	Icelandic	Danish Norwegian Swedish English German

Country & City	Principal Languages	Other Languages
Ireland Dublin	English Gaelic	
Italy Rome	Italian	
Liechtenstein Vaduz	German	
Luxembourg Luxembourg	French German	*
Malta Valletta	Maltese English	Italian
Monaco Monaco-Ville	French Monégasque	
The Netherlands Amsterdam	Dutch	English
Northern Ireland Belfast	English	
Norway Oslo	Norwegian	English

Country & City	Principal Languages	Other Languages
Poland		
Warsaw	Polish	
Poznan	Polish	German
Portugal		
Lisbon	Portuguese	
Romania		
Bucharest	Romanian	French
		German
		Hungarian
San Marino		
San Marino	Italian	
Scotland		
Edinburgh	English	Gaelic
Spain		
Madrid	Spanish	
Barcelona	Spanish	
	Catalan	
Bilbao	Spanish	Basque
Sweden		
Stockholm	Swedish	Finnish
		English
Switzerland		
Bern	German (Swiss)	German
		French
		Italian
Geneva	French	German
		Italian

Country & City	Principal Languages	Other Languages
Zurich	German (Swiss)	German French Italian
Union of Soviet Socialist Republics (USSR)†		
Armenian SSR (Yerevan)	Russian Armenian (Eastern)	
Azerbaijan SSR (Baku)	Russian Azerbaijani	Armenian (Eastern)
Byelorussian SSR (Minsk)	Russian Byelorussian	Polish
Estonian SSR (Tallin)	Russian Estonian	
Georgian SSR (Tbilisi)	Russian Georgian	Armenian (Eastern)
Kazakh SSR (Alma-Ata)	Russian Kazakh	Ukrainian
Kirgiz SSR (Frunze)	Russian Kirgiz	Ukrainian
Latvian SSR (Riga)	Russian Latvian	
Lithuanian SSR (Vilnius)	Russian Lithuanian	Polish
Moldavian SSR (Kishinev)	Russian Moldavian	Ukrainian

†The entries for the USSR are listed alphabetically by republic with the capital city of the republic in parentheses.

Country & City	Principal Languages	Other Languages
Russian SFSR (Moscow)	Russian	Armenian (Eastern) Ukrainian Tatar
Tadzhik SSR (Dushanbe)	Russian Persian (Tadzhik)	Uzbek
Turkmen SSR (Ashkhabad)	Russian Turkomen	Uzbek
Ukranian SSR (Kiev)	Russian Ukranian	
Uzbek SSR (Tashkent)	Russian Uzbec	
Vatican City	Italian	
Wales Cardiff	English Welsh	
Yugoslavia Belgrade	Serbo-Croatian	French German Macedonian Slovenian Albanian Hungarian

Near East

Afghanistan Kabul	Persian (Afghan) Pashto	French German Uzbek

Country & City	Principal Languages	Other Languages
Bahrain Manama	Arabic (Eastern)	
Bangladesh Dacca	Bengali	English
Bhutan Thimbu	Tibetan	
British Indian Ocean Territory	English French French Creole	
Ceylon (*see* Sri Lanka)		
Cyprus Nicosia	Greek Turkish	English
Egypt Cairo	Arabic (Eastern)	English French
Alexandria	Arabic (Eastern)	French Greek
India New Delhi	Hindi	Urdu Panjabi/Punjabi English
Bombay	Marathi Gujarati Hindi	English Urdu

Country & City	Principal Languages	Other Languages
Calcutta	Bengali	English
	Hindi	Oriya
		Assamese
Madras	Tamil	English
		Telugu
		Malayalam
		Kannada
Iran		
Tehran	Persian (Iranian)	French
Khorramshahr	Persian (Iranian)	French
	Arabic (Eastern)	
Tabriz	Persian (Iranian)	Kurdish
	Azerbaijani	French
		Russian
		Armenian (Eastern)
Iraq		
Baghdad	Arabic (Eastern)	Kurdish
Israel		
Jerusalem	Hebrew	English
	Arabic (Eastern)	French
		German
Tel Aviv	Hebrew	Arabic (Eastern)
		German
		Russian
		French
		Yiddish
		Judeo-Spanish
		English

Country & City	Principal Languages	Other Languages
Jordan Amman	Arabic (Eastern)	
Kuwait Kuwait	Arabic (Eastern)	Persian (Iranian)
Lebanon Beirut	Arabic (Eastern)	French Armenian (Western)
Maldive Islands Malé	Maldivian	
Nepal Kathmandu	Nepali	English Hindi Bhojpuri Newari
Oman Muscat	Arabic (Eastern)	
Pakistan Islamabad	Urdu Panjabi/Punjabi	English Lahnda Pashto
Lahore	Urdu Panjabi/Punjabi	English Lahnda
Karachi	Urdu Sindhi	English Gujarati

Country & City	Principal Languages	Other Languages
Qatar Doha	Arabic (Eastern)	
Saudi Arabia Jidda	Arabic (Eastern)	
Southern Yemen Aden	Arabic (Eastern)	Hindi Somali English
Sri Lanka (Ceylon) Colombo	Sinhala	Tamil English
Syria Damascus	Arabic (Eastern)	French English
Aleppo	Arabic (Eastern)	French Turkish Armenian (Western) Kurdish

Turkey
  Ankara
  Adana
	Turkish
	Turkish
		French
		Arabic (Eastern)
		Kurdish

Istanbul	Turkish	French Armenian (Western) Greek Judeo-Spanish

Country & City	Principal Languages	Other Languages
United Arab Emirates Abu Dhabi	Arabic (Eastern)	
Yemen Sanaa	Arabic (Eastern)	

Far East

Country & City	Principal Languages	Other Languages
American Samoa Pago Pago	English Samoan	
Australia Canberra	English	
Brunei Bandar Seri Begawan	Malay	Chinese (Hakka) English Iban
Burma Rangoon	Burmese	Chinese (Amoy) Chinese (Cantonese) Chinese (Mandarin) Karen (Sgaw) Karen (Pwo)

Cambodia
(*see* Kampuchea)

Country & City	Principal Languages	Other Languages
China (People's Republic of China)		
Beijing (Peking)	Chinese (Mandarin)	
Shanghai	Chinese (Mandarin)	Chinese (Fuchow)
	Chinese (Wu)	
Guangzhou	Chinese (Mandarin)	Chinese (Hakka)
(Canton)	Chinese (Cantonese)	Chinese (Swatow)
Nanning	Chinese (Mandarin)	Yao
	Chinese (Cantonese)	
	Zhuang	
China, Nationalist (Taiwan)		
Taipei	Chinese (Mandarin)	Chinese (Hakka)
	Chinese (Amoy)	Chinese (Fuchow)
Fiji		
Suva	Fijian	English
	Hindi	French
		Tamil
French Polynesia		
Papeete	Tahitian	
	French	
Gilbert Islands		
Tarawa	Gilbertese	
	English	
Guam		
Agagna	English	Ilocano
	Chamorro	

Country & City	Principal Languages	Other Languages
Hong Kong	Chinese (Cantonese)	Chinese (Mandarin) English
Indonesia Jakarta	Indonesian	Chinese (Amoy) Sundanese Javanese Dutch
Surabaya	Indonesian Javanese	Madurese Chinese (Amoy)
Japan Tokyo	Japanese	
Kampuchea (Cambodia) Phnom Penh	Cambodian	French Chinese (Cantonese) Chinese (Swatow) Vietnamese
Korea, North (Democratic People's Republic of Korea) Pyongyang	Korean	
Korea, South (Republic of Korea) Seoul	Korean	

Country & City	Principal Languages	Other Languages
Laos Vientiane	Lao	French Chinese (Cantonese) Chinese (Swatow) Vietnamese
Macao Macao City	Portuguese Chinese (Cantonese)	
Malaysia Kuala Lumpur	Malay	Chinese (Amoy) Chinese (Hakka) Chinese (Cantonese) Chinese (Mandarin) Chinese (Fuchow) English Tamil Javanese
Kuching	Malay Chinese (Hakka) Chinese (Fuchow)	English Chinese (Cantonese) Chinese (Mandarin) Iban Land Dyak
Mongolia Ulan Bator	Khalkha Mongolian	Russian
Nauru Nauru	Nauruan English	

Country & City	Principal Languages	Other Languages
New Caledonia Nouméa	French	
New Hebrides Vila	English French Pidgin English	
New Zealand Wellington	English	Maori
Northern Marianas Saipan	Chamorro	English
Okinawa Naha	Japanese Ryukyuan	English
Papua New Guinea Port Moresby	English Pidgin English	Motu
The Philippines Quezon City	Pilipino/Tagalog	English Spanish Ilocano Visayan (Cebuano) Chinese (Amoy) Chinese (Mandarin)
Pitcairn Islands	English	

Country & City	Principal Languages	Other Languages
Singapore Singapore	Malay Chinese (Amoy- Swatow) Chinese (Cantonese)	English Chinese (Mandarin) Chinese (Hakka) Tamil

Soloman Islands
  Honiara,
  Guadalcanal
	English
	Pidgin English	

Thailand Bangkok	Thai	Chinese (Swatow)
Tonga Nuku'alofa	Tongan English	
Trust Territory of the Pacific Islands	English	Trukese and eight other Micronesian languages
Tuvalu Funafuti	Ellicean Polynesian	English Samoan
Vietnam Hanoi	Vietnamese	Chinese (Mandarin) Chinese (Cantonese)
Saigon (Ho Chi Minh City)	Vietnamese	Chinese (Cantonese) French Cambodian

Country & City	Principal Languages	Other Languages
Wallis & Futuna Islands Mata-Utu	French	
Western Samoa Apia	Samoan English	

Africa

Country & City	Principal Languages	Other Languages
Algeria Algiers	Arabic (Western)	French Berber (Kabyle)
Angola Luanda	Kimbundu	Portuguese Umbundu Chokwe Kikongo
Benin (Dahomey) Porto Novo	Fon	French Yoruba
Botswana Gaberone	Tswana/Setswana	English
Burundi Bujumbura	Kirundi/Rundi	French Kinyarwanda Swahili/Kiswahili

Country & City	Principal Languages	Other Languages
Cameroon		
Yaoundé	Ewondo	French
	Wescos/English	English
	Creole	Duala
		Fang–Bulu
		Fula
Cape Verde Islands		
Praia	Portuguese	
	Portuguese Creole	
Central African Republic		
Bangui	Sango	French
	Banda	
	Gbaya	
Chad		
N'Djamena		French
	Arabic (Eastern)	Sara
Comoros		
Moroni	French	Malagasy
	Swahili/Kiswahili	
Congo		
Brazzaville	Lingala	French
	Kituba/Munukutuba	Kikongo
		Teke

Congo (Kinshasa)
(*see* Zaire)

Country & City	Principal Languages	Other Languages
Dahomey (*see* Benin)		
Djibouti Djibouti	Afar Somali	French Arabic (Eastern)
Equatorial Guinea Malabo	Fang	Spanish Bubi Yoruba
Ethiopia Addis Ababa	Amharic	English Oromo/Galla Italian
Asmara	Tigrinya Arabic (Eastern)	Amharic Italian Tigre
Gabon Libreville	Fang-Bulu	French
The Gambia Banjul	Mandingo (Malinke)	Fula English Wolof
Ghana Accra	Akan (Twi) Ga	English Ewe Hausa

Country & City	Principal Languages	Other Languages
Guinea		
Conakry	Susu Mandingo (Malinke) Fula	French
Guinea-Bissau		
Bissau	Portuguese Balante Fula	
Ivory Coast		
Abidjan	Baule	French Mandingo (Dioula)
Kenya		
Nairobi	Swahili/Kiswahili Kikuyu	English Luo Masai Kamba
Mombasa	Swahili/Kiswahili	English Arabic (Eastern)
Lesotho		
Maseru	Sotho/Sesotho	English
Liberia		
Monrovia	English Pidgin English	Bassa Vai Kpelle

Country & City	Principal Languages	Other Languages
Libya Tripoli	Arabic (Western)	Italian Berber (Djebel Nafusi)
Madagascar Antananarivo	Malagasy	French
Malawi Lilongwe	Chichewa/ Chinyanja/ Nyanja	English Yao Tumbuka
Mali Bamako	Mandingo (Bambara)	French Fula/Toucouleur
Mauritania Nouakchott	Arabic (Western)	French Fula Wolof Berber (Zenaga)
Mauritius Port-Louis	Mauritius Creole	English French Bhojpuri
Morocco Rabat	Arabic (Western)	French Berber (Tamazight)

Country & City	Principal Languages	Other Languages
Tangier	Arabic (Western)	Berber (Rif) French Spanish
Mozambique		
Maputo	Tsonga	Portuguese Tshwa
Beira	Chichewa/ Chinyanja/ Nyanja Shona	Portuguese
Mozambique	Makua	Portuguese Swahili/Kiswahili
Namibia		
Windhoek	Afrikaans English	German Ovambo Herero
Niger		
Niamey	Hausa Djerma-Songhai	Fula French Tamashek
Nigeria		
Lagos	Yoruba Pidgin English	English Hausa Igbo
Ibadan	Yoruba	Hausa English

Country & City	Principal Languages	Other Languages
Enugu	Igbo	English
		Hausa
		Efik
		Ijaw
Kano	Hausa	English
		Fula
		Kanuri
Republic of South Africa		
Capetown	Afrikaans	Zulu-Xhosa
Pretoria	Afrikaans	Zulu-Xhosa
	English	Sotho-Sesotho
		Tswana/Setswana
		Tsonga
Durban	English	Zulu-Xhosa
	Afrikaans	Gujarati
Réunion		
Saint-Denis	French	
	Réunion Creole	
Rwanda		
Kigali	Kinyarwanda	Kirundi/Rundi
		Swahili/Kiswahili
		French
Saint Helena		
Jamestown	English	

Country & City	Principal Languages	Other Languages
São Tomé & Príncipe São Tomé	Portuguese Portuguese Creole	
Sénégal Dakar	Wolof	French Fula/Toucouleur Serer Mandingo (Malinke) Diola Soninke Arabic (Western)
Seychelles Victoria	English French French Creole	
Sierra Leone Freetown	Krio	English Mende Temne
Somali Democratic Republic Mogadishu	Somali	Italian Arabic (Eastern) English

Country & City	Principal Languages	Other Languages
Sudan		
Khartoum	Arabic (Eastern)	Nubian
		Beja
		English
Juba	English	Dinka
	Arabic (Eastern)	Nuer
	Pidgin Arabic	Zande
	Bari	Toposa
		Lotuho
		Shilluk
Swaziland		
Mbabane	Swati/Siswati	English
		Zulu-Xhosa
		Afrikaans
Tanzania		
Dar es Salaam	Swahili/Kiswahili	Nyamwezi–Sukuma
		Gujarati
		English
Togo		
Lomé	Ewe	French
		Kabre
Tunisia		
Tunis	Arabic (Western)	French
Uganda		
Kampala	Luganda/Ganda	English
		Swahili/Kiswahili
		Acholi

Country & City	Principal Languages	Other Languages
Upper Volta		
Ouagadougou	Moré	Mandingo (Bambara)
		French
		Fula
Zaire		
Kinshasa	Lingala	French
	Kituba/Munukutuba	Kikongo
Bukuvu	Swahili/Kiswahili	French
	Amashi	
Lubumbashi	Swahili/Kiswahili	French
	Bemba/Cibemba	
	Lunda	
	Luba (Katanga)	
Zambia		
Lusaka	Chichewa/	English
	Chinyanja/	Tonga/Citonga
	Nyanja	
	Bemba/Cibemba	
Zimbabwe		
Salisbury	Shona	English
		Ndebele
		Chichewa/
		Chinyanja/
		Nyanja

Appendix 2
Pimsleur Language Programs & Date First Published

Greek	1963	Albanian	1994
French	1964	Ojibwe	1994
Latin American Spanish	1966	European Portuguese	1994
German	1967	Haitian Creole	1995
Twi	1971	Italian	1995
Hebrew	1982	Japanese	1995
Russian	1984	Swiss German	1995
Brazilian Portuguese	1990	Vietnamese	1995
Eastern Arabic	1991	Eastern Armenian	1996
English for Spanish	1991	Cantonese Chinese	1996
Mandarin Chinese	1991	Korean	1996
Czech	1993	Lithuanian	1996
Dutch	1993	Polish	1996
Ukrainian	1993	Egyptian Arabic	1997

Western Armenian	1997	Farsi Persian	2002
Croatian	1999	Turkish	2006
Danish	1999	Tagalog	2007
Hindi	1999	Hungarian	2008
Indonesian	1999	Dari Persian	2009
Irish	1999	Pashto	2010
Norwegian	1999	Urdu	2010
Swedish	1999	Modern Standard Arabic	2012
Romanian	2000	Finnish	2012
Swahili	2000	Punjabi	2012
Thai	2000	Castilian Spanish	2012

Pimsleur Language Programs
English as a Second Language

English for Spanish Speakers	1991
English for Japanese Speakers	1994
English for Mandarin Chinese Speakers	1996
English for French Speakers	1999
English for Hindi Speakers	1999
English for Italian Speakers	1999
English for Korean Speakers	1999
English for Russian Speakers	1999
English for Cantonese Chinese Speakers	2000
English for German Speakers	2000
English for Arabic Speakers	2001
English for Portuguese Speakers	2001
English for Vietnamese Speakers	2003
English for Haitian Speakers	2004
English for Farsi Persian Speakers	2006

Sources Used for "Languages of the World"

Almanac Publications. *The Official Associated Press Almanac*. New York: Almanac Publications, 1973.

Atlas Narodov Mira (Atlas of Peoples of the World). Moscow: Academy of Sciences of USSR, 1964.

British Information Services. *Britain's Associated States and Dependencies*. Norwich, England: Page Bros. Ltd., 1972.

Correspondence dated April 27, 1973, with Alain Chaillou, Director, Minister Plenipotentiary, French Embassy, New York.

Correspondence dated May 2, 1973, with Carlos Lamero, Director, Portuguese Tourist and Information Office, New York.

Foreign Service Institute. "List by Post of Useful Languages for U.S. Foreign Service Purposes at Overseas Posts."

Hayes, Curtis W., Orenstein, Jacob, and Gage, William W. *ABC's of Languages and Linguistics*. Silver Springs, MD: Institute of Modern Languages, 1977. Appendix.

Muller, Siegfried H. *The World's Living Languages*. New York: Frederick Ungar Publishing Co., 1964.

Rice, Frank A. (Ed.). *Study of the Role of Second Languages in Asia, Africa and Latin America*. Washington, D.C.: Center for Applied Linguistics, 1962.

Pimsleur.com
1-800-831-5497